KU-493-175

Sharing Expertise in Teacher Education

Mike Turner and Leslie Bash

CASSELL

London and New York

Cassell

Wellington House
125 Strand
London WC2R 0BB

370 Lexington Avenue
New York
NY 10017–6550

www.cassell.co.uk

© Mike Turner and Leslie Bash 1999

All rights reserved. No part of this publication may be reproduced or transmitted in any form or by any means, electronic or mechanical including photocopying, recording or any information storage or retrieval system, without prior permission in writing from the publishers.

First published 1999

British Library Cataloguing-in-Publication Data
A catalogue record for this book is available from the British Library.

ISBN 0–304–70289–7 (paperback)

Typeset by York House Typographic Ltd, London
Printed and bound in Great Britain by Redwood Books Ltd, Trowbridge, Wiltshire

CN 370.71

AN 8079

SHARING EXPERTISE IN TEACHER EDUCATION

Northern College
Library

NC02422

THE NORTHERN COLLEGE CANCELLED

LIBRARY

BARNSLEY

Also available from Cassell:

M. Booth, J. Furlong and M. Wilkin, *Partnerships in Initial Teacher Training*
C. Cullingford, *The Effective Teacher*
L. Haggarty, *New Ideas for Teacher Education*
J. Halliday, *Back to Good Teaching*
A. Hargreaves, *Changing Teachers, Changing Times*
A. Hargreaves and M. Fullan, *Understanding Teacher Development*
E. Hoyle and P. John, *Professional Knowledge and Professional Practice*
P. John Lesson, *Planning for Teachers*
T. Maynard (ed.), *An Introduction to Primary Mentoring*
R. Meighan, *A Sociology of Educating*
A. Pollard, *Reflective Teaching in the Primary School* (3rd edition)
A. Pollard, *Readings for Reflective Teaching in the Primary School*
J. Smyth (ed.), *Critical Discourses on Teacher Development*
L. Tickle, *The Induction of New Teachers*

Contents

Introduction

Our intention in producing this book is to review and comment on recent changes in the initial and continuing education of teachers in schools. We combine reviews of the current literature with previously unpublished research and make suggestions as to how some aspects of teacher education might develop and how it could be improved.

We have chosen to present our book as a series of connected chapters. Where this has led to some slight overlaps we apologize but we would argue that the viewpoints we take are sufficiently different to justify some repetition of focus.

The book is written to reflect the developmental order of teacher education, beginning in Chapter 1 with a review of recent changes in teacher education – tracing the influence of government policy on teacher education over the past twenty years and examining the impact of the most recent legislation on both initial training and in-service education for teachers.

We go on in Chapter 2 to look at the way in which teacher training and education courses are planned and validated under the latest regulations, paying close attention to the government's framework and its competences for teachers as well as the necessary negotiation and contractual arrangements that are implied by the necessity for partnerships in teacher training. The validation process is also looked at and commented on in the light of partnership and of school-centred teacher training.

Chapter 3 examines the way in which student teachers are supervised on their school-based teaching experiences and looks at the roles of university tutors and of supervising teachers, as well as giving students' views on the process. This chapter is based on a small-scale research project carried out by Leslie Bash and Ron Best.

We deal with induction in two separate chapters: Chapter 4 looks at primary school experiences of induction from all points of view and undertakes a thorough review of the literature in the area, whilst Chapter 5 offers the different perspectives of secondary teachers on induction. Chapter 5 has appended a short bibliography of recent publications on mentoring and induction which would be useful for serving teachers.

We move on to look at mentoring in Chapter 6. The chapter is based on research carried out by Mike Turner and colleagues and on recent publications in the area, and investigates ways in which mentoring can be linked with ongoing professional development for teachers and mentoring for women into senior management.

In Chapter 7 we look in some detail at ways in which continuing professional development can be provided for teachers through in-service education, both school- and university-based, and we make suggestions for future developments.

Chapter 8 looks at the way in which continuing professional development can be aided and indeed encouraged by the provision and maintenance of professional profiles which enable teachers to record and reflect on their formal and informal development. The chapter includes a discussion of the research evaluation of one LEA's professional development profile. The Teacher Training Agency's intention to provide new teachers with career entry profiles and to link them with its initiatives in training subject leaders, heads of departments and head teachers makes this a highly relevant and controversial area.

In Chapter 9 Mike Turner discusses his findings from a research tour of the United States during which he looked at the role of master teacher and of professional development schools in teacher training. It is his intention in this chapter to pull together some of the threads from teacher training, induction and mentoring, continuing professional development and school improvement programmes and to suggest some ways forward for teacher development in future.

It should be noted that our emphasis in this book is on the concept of teacher *education* but sometimes we follow the government and Teacher Training Agency's terminology and refer to initial teacher *training* (ITT).

Acknowledgements

Mike Turner wishes to thank Colin Lacey for his support as supervisor for his doctoral research on mentoring which, in many ways, provided the initial spur for this publication.

We are grateful to those students in the School of Education at Anglia Polytechnic University who participated in some of the research which is reported in this volume. We are also grateful to colleagues in schools and universities who have been willing to share their experiences with us. Finally, as always, we would like to thank our families for their invaluable support throughout the period of gestation of this project.

Chapter 1

Recent Changes in Teacher Education

> Professionals profess. They profess to know better than others the nature of certain matters, and to know better than their clients what ails them or their affairs. This is the essence of the professional idea and the professional claim. (Hughes, 1975, p. 249)

> It is not to disparage teacher training that we remark upon the fact that teachers still learn to teach by teaching. The teacher gets something from experience which is not included in his 'professional' courses, an elusive something which it is difficult to put between the covers of a book or to work up into a lecture. (Waller, 1932, p. 1)

Introduction

The late nineteenth- and twentieth-century industrialized world has witnessed the developing role of the 'professional' in public affairs as against that of the enthusiastic amateur. This has not been merely a concern with – or even a reference to – whether the activity is paid; it concerns rather the extent to which it is characterized by the application of specialist knowledge which is guarded by the professional fraternity for use in appropriate circumstances.

In the public services provided in many industrialized nations there has been an ideological shift away from statism (top-down, planned collective provision) towards consumerism (bottom-up, market-led). This has been reflected, for example, in the increased perceptions of power on the part of patients in relation to medical practice. Similarly, in teacher education, schools as the recipients of the 'end products' of the system would appear increasingly to be in a position to influence and shape the outcomes. More problematically, parents, who are assumed to be the consumers of schooling, remain somewhat peripheral to this process and, therefore, more problematic in relation to the sharing of expertise in teacher education. Conventionally, the notion of professionalism is connected with the assumption of expertise on the part of practitioners, the standards by which it is judged, and the locus of power in making decisions on standards and in controlling entry to the occupation. Never a profession in the traditional sense of the term, teaching in the public sector has generally been governed by the state, either centrally and/or locally with only a partial involvement at best by teachers themselves. Similarly with teacher education: it has had a public image of being an arm of the state, existing to prepare the next generation of classroom practitioners in publicly maintained schools (the nearest parallel might be nurse education and its relationship to the UK National Health Service).

Vocational training or professional education?

A simplistic view of teacher education in the UK – and elsewhere – in the last decade of the twentieth century might suggest the existence of diverse programmes of vocational training, based upon the inculcation of skills which are needed for a teacher to operate effectively in the classroom. According to this picture, teaching is much like any other occupation which requires the acquisition of a body of know-how in order that the job be undertaken. As the plumber possesses techniques related to pipe-bending and to getting central heating boilers to stay alight, so the teacher has acquired knowledge related to filling heads with facts, ensuring the ability to transfer those facts to paper, testing whether the process has been successful – and obtaining the requisite order in the classroom for the performance of these activities.

To the outsider, teaching has been seen as a fairly straightforward job, only complicated by threats of disruption from unruly charges, but amply compensated by short hours and long holidays. The status of the teacher has accordingly been somewhat problematic: super childminder (in the case of the large numbers of women in elementary/primary schools), literate/numerate tradesman (in the case of men working in elementary/primary/non-selective secondary schools) or scholar/academic (in the case of men and women working in elite secondary schools). This variability in the way in which teachers have been traditionally viewed has had an inevitable impact upon teacher education. Historically, the possession of a university degree was proof enough of the capacity to teach, since it merely confirmed the superior status of its holder who would appear to have already been imbued with a set of competencies related to the inculcation of knowledge to young charges of broadly similar status.

On the other hand, there were those who perceived teaching in terms of upward mobility but were unable to acquire or did not aspire to cap and gown – and there was a large number of young women drawn to teaching in the same way that others would be attracted to nursing and other 'helping' occupations. It was for this group that teacher training came into existence: a means by which prospective teachers could complete their formal education, acquire classroom competences, and generally be inducted into the culture of elementary/primary schooling. Following the 1944 Education Act, and the end of World War II, there was an expansion in the English teacher training college sector to take account of the extended secondary sector (the development of secondary modern schools for the mass of the population in addition to the elite grammar schools). At the same time, there was still no requirement on those who possessed a university degree to undergo professional training – a situation which continued through to the 1970s.

It was fairly clear that the professional apartheid demarcating grammar school/public school degree-holding teachers from certificated primary/secondary modern school teachers was going to be challenged as a result of diverse changes taking place in education and in the world outside. To a significant extent this would also manifest itself in teacher education. The traditional hierarchy characterizing teachers did not look safe in an age of transition from ascription to meritocracy. What was more, the expansion of opportunities for higher education in the UK, alongside the corollary of credential inflation, meant that a first degree was bound to become the minimum qualification for entry to the profession, even if that degree was vocationally based. The eventual arrival of an all-graduate teaching force was no more than a recognition of a changed socio-economic climate which had impacted upon the western industrialized world. At the same time, though, it also seemed to suggest that all teachers should have a status commensurate with that of lawyers, doctors and others deemed to belong to a traditional 'profession': teachers were to receive a professional and academic *education* rather than a period of vocational *training*.

It is noteworthy that the situation in other countries varies considerably with regard to the kind of qualification deemed appropriate for teaching. For example, as late as 1990 in Israel, less than 17 per cent of primary school teachers were graduates, having received their training in 'non-academized' teacher training colleges. On the other hand, high school teachers possessed university degrees in specialized subjects and became qualified after following a postgraduate teaching certificate programme. However, there have been moves since the 1970s towards the upgrading of the educational level of Israeli teacher training colleges with two-year programmes expanded to three years, the 'academizing' of some institutions, and a small number given authorization to award B.Ed. and B.TecEd. degrees (Guri-Rozenblit, 1990, p. 226).

It is clear that this state of affairs was never entirely accepted by all. Teaching has seldom been seen to possess the mystique attached to the law, medicine or the priesthood. Rather, it is an activity which requires the possession of varying degrees of knowledge and the skills with which to transmit it to the young. In an era of ideological turbulence, global economic shift and increased international competition, the control of education systems and those who work in them is judged to be of the utmost importance. Hence the importance of measurable skills and competences rather than of broad-based liberal academic study. Moreover, the emphasis increasingly given to the role of the consumer and the 'rolling back' of the state has legitimized a fundamental change in the process of teacher education.

Such change has highlighted the tension between observable behaviours on the part of teachers, which can be subjected to 'objective' assessment, and the possession of knowledge and understanding which may have a more indirect relationship with practice. It is often seen as a tension between technical expertise and unsubstantiated belief, deriving from ideologically bound 'theory'. To a very large degree, a 'technicist' model of teacher education/training has appeal to schools who have increasing responsibility for the entire business, from the delivery of the National Curriculum to financial decisions concerning the hiring of teachers and the purchase of resources. Schools have established cultures into which newly qualified teachers and those in the midst of their professional preparation must be inducted, and the technicist model may be the most appropriate.

The shaping of policy

We now arrive at the very core of the discourse which has dominated policy-making in teacher education during the last fifteen years in the UK. In mirroring the broader debate on education, it is beset with ideological certitude, contradictions and conflicts of interest. In brief, some of the key changes emanating from this discourse and implemented by central government have been:

- a fundamental challenge to the teacher education 'establishment';
- an emphasis on competencies;
- a move towards school-centred/school-provided training;
- a concentration of decision-making powers at the centre;
- a continuing penetration by the ideology of the market.

Where policy-makers sense that the tide is ready to turn in the direction which has been decided upon by influential thinkers (as in the case of Sheila Lawler with the Conservative government of the 1980s/1990s), they frequently seek legitimation through some sort of comparison with other state systems. As Cowen asserts: 'The probability that other countries are indeed doing something better in education is now part of the public discourse of English politicians and the mass media' (1990, p. 45). This 'grass is greener' approach, argues Cowen (p. 47) has permeated English educational policy-making for the last three decades or more, and has more often than not focused upon the United States. Thus, the status of teacher education was progressively raised throughout the 1960s and 1970s in the English system, with incorporation into multi-faculty establishments – higher education colleges, polytechnics, universities. This was accompanied by the eventual achievement of graduate qualifications for all teachers, notably the four-year bachelor of education honours degree. The process of cross-national transfer was quite blatant and was to continue through to the 1980s and 1990s, when the central state in the UK took significantly greater control of the entire process of education – including teacher training.

It was the convergence of a number of concerns, reflecting clear ideological perspectives, which prompted swift changes in teacher education. The first concern was the supposed influence of unbridled 'progressivism' in education, reflected in the dominance of teacher education by the training institutions and their emphasis upon theory, notably the social sciences, whose place had been assured in the preparation of teachers during the 1960s. By the end of the decade, sociology in particular had emerged as the leading discipline, viewed by some as the promoter of radicalism among students, challenging accepted pedagogical traditions and, indirectly at least, fostering anarchy in schools. While tabloid newspaper headlines screamed disorder and mayhem in the country's classrooms during the 1970s, the reality was in fact rather less dramatic with probably a majority of schools continuing to operate in a relatively conservative fashion. English and mathematics, as core subjects of the yet to be born National Curriculum, were generally being taught in both primary and secondary schools along conventional lines. Likewise, teachers, generally speaking, continued to operate in a traditional manner and those entering, or preparing to enter, the profession were very soon inducted into the culture of the school and its established set of norms and values. Yet, this was not how it appeared to an increasing number of, mostly, but not exclusively, right-wing critics of educational theory and practice as typified by the Black Papers – and to the then Prime Minister, James Callaghan, in his 1976 Ruskin College speech. Few were surprised that an incoming Conservative government in 1979 with a 'radical' agenda would set about not only an overhaul of the school system but also the system for the preparation of teachers. The fact that the new government was able to do this was not simply due to a parliamentary majority but also, in no small part, to a recognition of difficulties, dilemmas and conflicts from within the education profession.

The role of the school in the preparation of teachers

In its efforts to combat the power and influence of the colleges and universities in the preparation of teachers, the UK central government has given schools, in principle, a central role in initial teacher training. This, of course, has placed the traditional providers of initial training in an uncomfortable position: while the judgement of schools regarding the ability to perform adequately in the classroom is to be taken seriously this does not necessarily mean that they should be in control of the entire training process. Training institutions after all have allegedly possessed a considerable amount of expertise which has allowed them to provide students with a broad overview of pedagogy and educational issues. The relative universalism of training institutions as against the particularism of an individual school guards against a narrowly conceived perspective on teaching and yet there is the recognition of the importance of the accumulated wisdom of practitioners.

On the other hand, not all schools have the wish to participate more fully in initial training programmes, because of time constraints and the consequences of policy change related to the curriculum. However, at secondary level, school-based initial training is now well established following Circular 9/92 (DFE, 1992) and enquiries have been undertaken into the efficacy of moves in this direction, among them a case study of a one-year postgraduate certificate in education (PGCE) school-based programme in Southern England (Blake et al., 1996). While the study showed general endorsement of moves towards more school-based secondary ITT some concerns were nonetheless voiced on the part of students, teachers and HE tutors. Apart from the known difficulties related to the time and resources available to schools for initial training (in particular for adequate and effective mentoring), a more fundamental anxiety was expressed about the nature and balance of the overall student experience. On the one hand there was the disengagement of HE from the business of supervision of practical teaching and, on the other, teachers believed that they should not have the sole responsibility for the training process since it would lead to a reduction in 'that critical edge about teaching which results from systematic, HE-based professional work' (Blake et al., 1996, p. 34).

Elsewhere, parallels have been sought in the notion of the teaching hospital as a centre of excellence in relation to the transmission of good medical practice and as a context for innovation and creativity; in the context of teacher training, this is the professional development school (PDS). In such establishments, the boundaries between university teachers and teachers in schools are less heavily drawn. Not only is the PDS seen as a centre of excellence as far as its own pedagogical practices are concerned, and thus an ideal context for 'clinical' practice, but its teaching staff are also viewed as having sufficient expertise to contribute to the overall programme of initial training. Likewise, university tutors may spend time as teachers in the PDS, updating their understanding and knowledge in a practical educational context, although, as a study of one Canadian PDS project suggested (Cook and McClean, 1995, p. 320), some of the taken-for-granted assumptions of university staff need to be challenged. This is especially important where university teachers are there for only a limited period and are not fully appreciative of the school culture.

Evaluation of policy

The shaping of policy with respect to teacher education, as with much else, has not come about simply as a consequence of the imposition of ideology. Neither 'conspiracy' nor 'cock-up' theories seem adequate explanations for the emergence of new structures and processes. There is, however, some strength to the argument that it was partly the failure of the teaching profession to develop a coherent and co-ordinated view of its role and function in relation to children, learning, parents, and society at large which has enabled the policy-makers at national level to step into the breach in an incisive manner. While the final responsibility for licensing teachers in England and Wales has always rested with central government, it is only within recent times that this has extended to the prescription of course content in initial training. Prescription of content will, it is anticipated, result in a unified teaching profession which has undergone similar training, with an emphasis upon the same set of competencies, and is thoroughly prepared for the implementation of the National Curriculum. The progression in central government policy is now summarized below.

Date	Event	Significance
1976	James Callaghan's Ruskin College speech	Criticism of school system. Central government should be more closely involved.
1984	DES Circular 3/84	Council for the Accreditation of Teacher Education (CATE) established: all ITT programmes to meet CATE criteria, with increased emphasis on classroom practice.
1986	White Paper: Better Schools	Call for raising of standards and national curriculum.
1988	Education Reform Act	National Curriculum established → new requirements for ITT programmes.
1992	DFE Circular 9/92	Secondary PGCE programmes to be school-based.
1993	DFE Circular 14/93	New criteria for primary programmes which should be planned in conjunction with primary schools.
1994	Teacher Training Agency (TTA) established	To fund and control pattern of ITT, including accreditation – consortia of schools to be considered as ITT providers (school-centred initial teacher training – SCITT). CATE wound up.
1997	DfEE Circular 10/97	ITT national 'standards' established.
1998	DfEE Circular 4/98	ITT National Curriculum for core subjects set out.

It would appear, at least superficially, that teachers are now central to the future of British society: they carry a heavy responsibility and, accordingly, should be trained in a manner which ensures the successful transmission of the core skills and knowledge which will return the country to a position of economic and political prominence. Yet, this kind of rhetoric, designed to place moral pressure upon teachers, does not appear to be matched by the status and power which is ascribed to the profession. On the contrary, teachers – and, most significantly, teacher trainers – have consistently been on the receiving end when it comes to the placement of blame for 'falling standards', classroom disorder, etc. The result is the creation of a centralized machinery which has built into it mechanisms for assessment, testing and quality control.

Thus, a prescriptive National Curriculum plus a system of national testing and assessment (constructed by the School Curriculum and Assessment Authority (SCAA), now the Qualifications and Curriculum Authority (QCA)) is to be delivered by a teaching force trained on the basis of measured competencies. The new, semi-privatized inspection body – the Office for Standards in Education (OFSTED) – exists to ensure the maintenance and promotion of teaching quality and, accordingly, descends upon schools and training institutions at frequent intervals for this purpose. The upshot is a more or less permanent concern to meet the demands of the quality controllers – which, for teacher training establishments, means, in addition, the Teacher Training Agency.

This current state of policy might be further understood if change in other national systems of teacher education is considered. The move towards a highly regulated, school-based, competency-driven approach is by no means universal, although the pressure to quantify performance achievement in practical classroom skills is partly the outcome of a market orientation towards education which has impacted upon a number of nation states. The downfall of Communism in Eastern Europe at the end of the 1980s and the continued privatization of previously state-run industries in the West have bolstered a free-market view of the world. On the other hand, in the UK at least, the market has been seemingly tempered by the introduction of a mass of regulatory machinery, with the supposed purpose of protecting consumers from the consequences of producers' actions pursued purely in their own interests. In 1989, non-university higher education institutions were freed from local authority control, but only to be subjected to regulation/quality control in a much more centralized manner – and, as we have seen, especially in the area of teacher training.

However, the position may vary from that in the UK in those nation states which are characterized by rather different histories. Despite the continued turbulence in the former Warsaw Pact countries and other regions of Eastern Europe, and even the return to popularity of communist/socialist parties, there is an understandable reluctance to build centralized structures to regulate social affairs. The new-found freedoms of the 1990s are as apparent in the world of education as they are in other public spheres. In Hungary, for example, higher education institutions concerned with initial teacher education (universities and teacher training colleges) are faced with the prospect of training/re-training teachers for the implementation of the

National Basic Curriculum (NBC) in September 1998 (Besançon et al., 1996, section III B). Although, in contrast to the National Curriculum of England and Wales, the Hungarian NBC is a loose framework within which schools will be able to develop particular curricula to suit local circumstances, it nonetheless offers a challenge to teachers and teacher educators which requires them to relinquish a degree of autonomy. Essentially, though, it will be the higher education institutions themselves who will make the decisions regarding curricular content of initial training and re-training programmes – and not central government, quangos, or other national organizations.

Conclusion

Although the last decade or so has witnessed a plethora of changes which has affected both the structure and content of teacher education in England and Wales, the expectation that a different central government would create a period of stability (or even reverse certain policies) has not been met. While party political ideological distinctions increasingly appear to be a part of the distant past, and there is a good deal of consensus on education in general (albeit contained within a much more right-wing frame of reference), significant aspects of teacher education remain contested. The chapters which follow explore some of these aspects, noting innovations, debates and continuing questions.

Chapter 2

Programme Planning and Validation

Introduction

Until relatively recently, in England and Wales, programmes of initial teacher education were planned much in the same way as other higher education programmes, with some attention paid to the minimal demands of the central state. The planning process was largely in the hands of teacher educators, some of whom had been classroom practitioners themselves, while others were in the main academics. This was especially in evidence during the 1960s and 1970s when teacher training became transformed by its inclusion within the higher education sector, when colleges of education were associated with universities through the processes of validation and assessment. It meant that universities that had departments of education, mainly concerned with postgraduate initial training, higher degrees and research, also established 'institutes of education'. These were essentially consortia of training colleges whose certificate and, later, degree (B.Ed.) programmes were those of the parent universities and, generally speaking, were allegedly constructed and validated without too much fuss or rigour. Rather more cynically, validation was seen as a 'back of a cigarette packet' process that would be finally sealed over a glass of sherry. This was seen to contrast with the stricter and more gruelling validating procedures of the Council for National Academic Awards (CNAA) which was to become much more in evidence as the colleges gained autonomy, often through mergers with others or with existing polytechnics.

By the late 1970s, the process of programme planning and validation for initial teacher education was varied and in a state of flux, reflecting some of the ideological conflicts that had manifested themselves on both the educational and national political stages. Autonomy and academic freedom vied with the demands for uniformity and 'high standards' and a need to ensure that the next generation was adequately prepared for an increasingly competitive world. The centralizing tendencies of the new Conservative administration after 1979 made themselves felt, as regards initial teacher education, in 1984 with the creation of the Council for the Accreditation of Teacher Education (CATE). On the other hand, the advent of the National Curriculum and the move towards 'competency' have arguably placed schools in a stronger position in relation to the entire process of programme planning and validation. Despite the fact that higher education institutions were still to retain overall control, the support for 'school-based' approaches to the basic aspects of training meant that the process was to become an increasingly shared activity. Schools had now become legitimate authors of their own destinies: training institutions surely had only limited competence in making decisions as to the criteria for effective teaching. The latter could not be expected to design programmes to deliver the kinds of practical knowledge and understandings required for satisfactory classroom performance without the real participation of the schools themselves.

The Teacher Training Agency: walking the political tightrope?

Some may wish to ponder the apparent contradictions between two separate policies. On the one hand, schools were to be subjected to increasingly rigorous inspections as a result of the perceived lack of competence on the part of a significant number of their teachers. On the other, they were also regarded as being perfectly adequate to the task of training the next generation of classroom practitioners, and the Teacher Training Agency, which replaced CATE, has gone even further down the road of school involvement in initial teacher education through the establishment of school-centred (SCITT) programmes. In other words, the process of programmme planning and validation was no longer the monopoly of higher education institutions and therefore such institutions were challenged to reflect upon their role. The emphasis had shifted to the process of licensing – the authority to grant qualified teacher status, and the central state had demonstrated that it had powers of patronage relating to who should be regarded as the main licensing authority – either the training institutions or the schools. If the emphasis was to be placed on the latter it would be largely the consequence of a desire to curb the alleged power of the universities to prescribe the content of initial teacher education programmes along critical lines which could challenge traditional pedagogy, rather than of a recognition of the knowledge and expertise held by classroom teachers.

   At the time of writing, the Teacher Training Agency (1997) published a consultation document on revised requirements for initial training courses which placed significant emphasis upon 'partnership with schools' (p. 7), stating that all non-school trainers should ensure that 'schools are fully and actively involved in the planning and delivery of ITT ... The full partnership should regularly review and evaluate the training provided' (3.1.1). Yet 3.1.3 (p. 7) notes that there must be procedures 'for the deselection of schools' which do not meet set criteria and, further on, this is reaffirmed by 4.1.4 (p. 8), which states that 'only those schools and teachers who can offer appropriate training and support for trainees are [to be] used to provide ITT'.

So, once again, there is a need to tread carefully when discussing the issue of partnership in teacher education. Even the TTA, the agency charged with the implementation of central government policy, is apparently aware that not every school possesses the required attributes to be able to participate on an equal footing with higher education institutions (HEIs) in the process of programme construction. The tension between the civil service function of a government agency such as the TTA and the professional role retained by those who work for that agency will not usually manifest itself in an open manner unless individuals are prepared to risk their positions. The tension is more likely to work itself out in the texts of documents, at the level of policy implementation, and in the conversations between officers of the agency and professionals in the field. Hence, it is also likely that the process of planning programmes of initial training, against the backcloth of a centrally driven partnership policy, will ultimately be a pragmatic affair. This may be an overly optimistic view but anecdotal evidence suggests, on the basis of recent TTA visits to HEIs, that the implementation of teacher education policy in this respect is not to be bureaucratically imposed, however much it may be desired by education ministers from the two major political parties.

Programme content

This raises the issue of what exactly should be the content of initial teacher education programmes. Conventionally, schools are supposed to have held training institutions in relatively low regard, viewing them as the purveyors of uninformed rarefied theory which had little relevance for the classroom. This was usually enshrined in the 'induction' given to newly qualified teachers which went along the lines of: 'You can forget all that college stuff – you need to learn how to deal with the real world.' Undoubtedly, this teacher-derived populism has resonated with many parents who have tended to view schooling in crude, commonsense terms – a combined process of child containment and instillation of numeracy and literacy – and it has been readily taken on board by a central government bent on dismantling the 'educational establishment'. What began with the critique of 'progressive' schooling provided by the Black Papers of the late 1960s and early 1970s, continuing through the Great Debate and culminating in the radical upheavals of the 1980s and 1990s, was bound eventually to impact upon the world of teacher education. It seemed obvious that having sufficiently tamed the teaching profession through the imposition of the National Curriculum, national testing and OFSTED, some recovery in the standing of the teaching profession might be achieved if it could play a crucial role in changing the process of initial training. Teachers would be in a powerful position to counter the 'irrelevance' of 'theory' through an appeal to tried and tested pedagogy rooted in the accumulated experience of practitioners.

Evaluation

It was always going to be a great deal easier, at least in principle, with English secondary teacher education programmes, where the postgraduate route has predominated in recent years. Since such students are presumed to possess suffi-cient subject knowledge through their undergraduate studies, much turns on the quality of training in relation to methods of teaching. The schools were seen by central government to possess the necessary knowledge and experience in this area and, accordingly, postgraduate secondary initial training programmes are required to be entirely school-based, with schools fully involved in the planning process. To what extent this is related to the view which prevailed until around 1970, that a first degree in a liberal arts subject was the main qualification and a teaching certificate, though desirable, was not mandatory, is debatable. It would not be straying far from the truth to say that the transmission model of pedagogy remains alive and well in secondary schools.

It was therefore reasonable to suppose that the first foray into school-*centred* teacher training was to be in the secondary field. SCITT was to be based upon consortia of schools which were to be given the opportunity to design, organize and provide school-based programmes for graduates and would lead directly to Qual-ified Teacher Status (QTS) (OFSTED, 1995, p. 1). During 1993/1994, funding for initial SCITT programmes was paid directly to six secondary consortia by the (then) Department for Education at a flat rate of £4,000 per student teacher. In all, 150 students were recruited, with five schools offering courses which were to be validated by HEIs, and one school offering its own qualification leading to QTS (OFSTED, 1995, p. 2). (This last point is of some interest since HEIs may still offer significant 'cultural capital' when compared with the image of QTS being awarded by a group of schools.) Since the SCITT scheme embodies much that is central to government policy on initial teacher education, OFSTED's assessment of this first cohort is somewhat mixed. The quality of training varied between consortia and difficulties were experienced in the co-ordination of training within consortia (OFSTED, 1995, p. 5), while the content and quality of programmes both in professional studies and subject training were sometimes less than satisfactory (OFSTED, 1995, p. 6).

Conclusion

On the basis of such evaluations, higher education institutions might feel a certain degree of satisfaction in that they are probably unlikely to lose their role in the process of planning and validation. It is also probable that the majority of schools will be content with this state of affairs so long as teachers feel that their legitimate concerns regarding the quality and content of initial training are noted. This, perhaps, is of less significance than the disquiet which surrounds the role of the state and the extent to which it attempts to counter the influence of the 'educational establishment' in this process. In general, there has been a global process of disengagement by the state from the provision of goods and services but, paradoxically, there has been in many cases a strengthening of the state's grip on knowledge production, since that is now perceived to be at the heart of a country's competitive position in the world. It follows, therefore, that if the state is able to control the content of the teacher training curriculum it will have a knock-on effect for the entire education system.

However, in the case of the UK, the state has increasingly managed to distance itself from its own activities. Much of national policy implementation has been devolved in recent years to state agencies which appear to have a degree of autonomy and to quasi-autonomous non-governmental organizations (Quangos), staffed by non-civil servant government nominees (e.g. the Qualifications and Curriculum Authority – QCA). This has been a piecemeal process which has resulted in a certain degree of tension between such agencies with contradictory consequences. In many respects, OFSTED is the more important state agency since it wields power both in the schools and in the teacher training establishments in a specific grass-roots manner, while the Teacher Training Agency operates at a higher level. The absence of a general teaching council representing all teachers in schools and in HEIs, akin to the General Medical Council or Law Society, both of which denote the self-governing nature of the respective professions, precludes a coherent, united approach to the planning process. Such a council might help make discussion of partnership less problematic. As it is, the shape of initial teacher education programmes will continue to be the outcome of negotiations between the various parties within the general pattern of constraints set by OFSTED, the TTA and QCA.

Chapter 3

Supervision of Students

Introduction

Whether teacher training is approached from the standpoint of the primacy of 'grand theory', or from a position which extols the virtues of classical 'apprenticeship', there does appear, nonetheless, to be something of a consensus regarding the core of initial professional education: practical experience in the classroom. This is, however, the single most problematic aspect of programmes of initial teacher education since it calls into question the exact nature of the teaching and learning process which characterizes this aspect of professional preparation. Conventionally, this has been known as 'supervision' and yet it is a remarkably unexplored issue, taken for granted by college-based teacher trainers – those traditionally charged with the duty of guiding students through what might be regarded as the most stressful aspect of the entire process.

The concept of supervision, while retained in the case of students undergoing courses of initial training, has, in the past, been invoked with regard to employed teachers, suggesting, beyond all measure of doubt, a relationship of power. Systems of school inspection across both time and space have had the result of varying degrees of supervision over the work of teachers: from friendly advice through to explicit commands in respect of teaching methods, classroom organization, behaviour management, etc. Supervision of students has, to some extent, mirrored the changing modes of inspection, with many tutors formerly 'being there' in the classroom, allegedly observing the student at work, finally making comments of a platitudinous kind and then hurriedly leaving to make a flying visit to the next trainee. While schools, with their continuing, closer contact with students as compared with college-based tutors, were allowed some degree of influence in the assessment process, they generally had no role in supervision.

In short, observation of students was traditionally the realm of college and university lecturers, with teachers usually offering advice less formally. As far as the position in England and Wales is concerned, this has now changed with the demands of DFE Circular 14/93 and the development of school-based and school-centred teacher training. As we shall see, teachers are now involved with the observation of students, as part of the formal process of supervision, throughout their training and, accordingly, there will be some exploration of the issues associated with this process.

It is important, at this stage, to examine ways in which colleges and universities have responded to the implementation of the National Curriculum. It is equally clear that whatever else happened this was bound to impact upon the manner in which students planned and prepared for block periods of practical teaching experience. As classroom teachers have had to change their mode of practice, so they may also have become more willing to share their ideas and develop expertise in respect of the National Curriculum and in the assessment of children's learning. In this context, there will be some exploration of teacher involvement in helping students with the organization and planning of learning activities.

In our examination of new approaches to the supervision of practical teaching experience we have so far offered some general observations and an outline of the changes at national policy level and their mode of implementation. However, prior to this, some teacher training institutions had already put limited schemes into operation whereby schools had been invited to participate in the student supervision process. An evaluation of one such scheme is summarized below.

School-based supervision in primary initial training: a pilot study

In one English university, during 1992, a group of students on a four-year primary Bachelor of Education course were invited to participate in a pilot school-based supervision scheme (Bash and Best, 1992). Although the students were in the second year of their programme this was to be their first block period of practical teaching experience. It should be noted that this was perceived by students and tutors as a significant change to their programme and, accordingly, students selected for inclusion in the pilot study were briefed some weeks prior to their block period of practical teaching experience. While this meeting was not recorded, the tutors who met with the students at that time reported that a number expressed anxiety over their participation. This anxiety seemed to have stemmed from:

1. the fact that the news of their selection came relatively late, after they had undertaken pre-practice visits during which they (and the schools) believed that the practice was to be conventionally supervised;
2. a concern that they might be disadvantaged in comparison with their peers undertaking conventional practices;
3. a feeling of simply being treated differently;
4. a loss of the security of regular contact with a university tutor.

Student evaluation of the scheme

While most students reported, at the meeting, that tutors attempted to allay such fears, a number were clearly still very apprehensive. Nonetheless the pilot scheme went ahead and was followed up by an evaluation session immediately after the period of practical teaching experience had finished. Here, students were asked to discuss their experiences with a tutor who had not previously been associated with the scheme. The following summarizes the main points which emerged from the discussion:

- There was a recognition that an evaluation of experiences during the scheme would be a difficult task because, as this had been the students' first practice, they had nothing with which to compare it. However, generally positive comments were made with the experience providing 'good practice' in 'supportive environments'.

- There were some stark contrasts between the ways in which different schools approached the practice. One head teacher set out her requirements very clearly, and made it clear that these requirements were not negotiable, while others were less directive and (apparently) less clear about the expectations of the school.

- Teachers' attitudes also varied. Some were directive; others preferred to let the students try their own methods, make their own mistakes and (hopefully) learn from them. One teacher was described as 'interfering', another as 'knowing it all' : 'she "*knew*" there was only one way to do anything!' One student described how she 'felt scared at the beginning', but said that her class teacher had been very good, had given her all the support she needed, and had built up her confidence. Others seemed to confirm similar experiences. Students concluded that a supportive teacher was crucial, given the relative lack of tutor involvement.

- Teachers played their role in a variety of ways. Some interchanged, and observed each other's students, which was welcomed because it gave the student useful feedback from two perspectives. Some teachers adhered rigidly to the requirement by arranging one one-hour formal observation each week while others did not and saw their one-hour observations consisting of shorter periods of time, sometimes woven into their normal classroom activity. Some appeared to have taken this requirement as merely a general indication, and undertook their observations quite informally. Interestingly, no student voiced objection to any of these approaches although there were sometimes negative comments regarding individuals. One head teacher was felt to be formidable and, during her observations, she 'had a face like thunder'. She was reported to have given no direct feedback, although positive comments were later relayed via the class teacher. However, in this case, the students did not seem to feel they were being treated badly.

- Practice varied also in respect of the files students have been conventionally required to keep, setting out curriculum planning, evaluations, records of children's learning, etc. Some schools were unclear about the university requirements. In some cases, the head teacher and/or class teacher checked the file meticulously; in other cases they were quite casual about it. Teachers varied from seeing the file as a very formal and systematic document, to seeing it as a working document which needed only to meet the practical needs of the student.

- Students came to believe that their teachers obtained a much better picture of them as classroom practitioners than did university tutors, because the class teacher was 'there all the time' and saw the student continuously in a wide variety of teaching situations. Class teachers were also seen as more helpful and understanding because they face similar problems to those of the student, but on a daily basis. Assessment of the tutors ranged from 'brilliant' through 'helpful' to 'useless', 'gave no concrete advice or practical tips'.

- There was a minority view that students felt isolated from the university because they had little contact with their tutors. Others reported, however, that this was their preference.

- Students seemed to appreciate, in particular, opportunities to sit down with class teachers and work together in planning a schedule of teaching and observation (both of the teaching practice class and other classes), including periods of team-teaching.

- Questions were raised regarding the choice of schools, with some students suggesting that monetary reward on the part of some schools might be a key factor. They noted that at least one school felt it needed more information about the students, their prior experience, subject expertise, etc.

- At various points in practice, the students had made contact with peers being supervised in the conventional way. They believed that they had gained a great deal more from the practice, in the form of practical help and useful evaluative feedback from the teacher, than had their peers.

Tensions and dilemmas

Despite the generally positive views on the part of students regarding this pilot scheme, some crucial issues surfaced during the student feedback session.

- On the one hand, if teachers were too prescriptive and did not allow students to experiment, adopt their own approaches and make their own mistakes, there was a feeling of constraint on their professional development. On the other hand, students appreciated the need for guidance and were critical of teachers who were too laissez-faire in their relationships with them.

- Class teachers were seen as more helpful, understanding and practically supportive than tutors, and it was therefore natural for them to undertake the assessment of the student. However, this also meant that it was seen as more difficult for students to challenge the views of teachers, depart from their advice or try approaches which, it was felt, would meet with disapproval. Consequently, supervision/assessment by a university tutor was perceived as a useful screen or buffer, with appropriate feedback and support.

- It was viewed as entirely appropriate for a class teacher to undertake observation while carrying out normal activities in the classroom (e.g. hearing children read), although, for reasons already stated, there were benefits in having another teacher undertake the observation.

The future

Finally, the students, in response to whether the university should continue with school-based supervision and whether any changes should be recommended, made the following points:

- There was, in general, a positive attitude towards the scheme and, while admitting that they had only indirect evidence of traditional experience, they were clear that they felt the arrangements of the pilot scheme to be superior.
- The university should be careful in its selection of schools used for such a scheme.
- The schools – meaning class teachers/supervisors and head teachers – need to be more clearly briefed, with stricter guidelines about university expectations of the students (including the teaching load required, the standards of assessment to be employed, etc.) to ensure comparability across schools.
- Students still needed a university tutor, especially if there arose particular issues connected with the school. Such a tutor might be someone already known to, and compatible with, the student.
- There was agreement that university tutors should visit students on more than one occasion, commencing at an early stage in the practice. It was also seen as crucial that such visits should be at times when the students were available for discussion.
- While schools should undertake the assessment of students, the university should moderate this to ensure equality of treatment. Variability in school cultures and environments demanded this.

Tutors' perspectives

A variety of initial perceptions on the part of tutors was derived from diverse data, including comments made at a meeting immediately after initial visits to the pilot schools and at a second meeting at the conclusion of the practice. At the first meeting, tutors reported on the reception they had received from each of the schools with which they made contact, and especially during their pre-practice visit.

Schools varied in the degree of confidence with which they accepted the responsibility. They varied in their clarity as to role expectations of the teacher and the tutor, the status of the 60/40 per cent guideline on teaching/non-teaching time, the competencies to be expected of students, the requirements of the file, and so on.

A number of the issues raised were not unique to the pilot scheme. For example, one school was concerned that the student's style might not match the school's preferred style, and there was a concern that students might be expected to emulate the model of their teacher/mentor, and thus not be given sufficient opportunity to develop their own approaches.

Some interesting – and intriguing – differences in the organization of the supervision were noted. These included:

- two class teachers supervising their own students, but moderating each other in order to resolve role-conflict in respect of assessment and support;
- a triangular arrangement where the head teacher supervised the deputy's student, and the deputy supervised the class teacher's student;
- the head teacher simply asserting that she would supervise the students;
- two class teachers to supervise, monitored by the head teacher;
- the deputy head to supervise but the class teachers to be the main source of guidance and support.

These and other possible patterns should be compared, evaluated and discussed by the university with a view to recommending one or more to schools. It should also be stated, at this stage, that a minority of schools which were approached were critical of school-based supervision. One school withdrew on the principle that the training of teachers was not its job. The response of a second school raised warning signals immediately. Here, the concern was with the doubtful morality of collaborating in 'teacher-training on the cheap', and there was a strong objection to the token payment of £20 per student per week which was seen as derisory.

Tutors reported that schools varied in their mode of decision-making regarding whether they should participate in the scheme, and how the practice/supervision would be organized. Thus, schools may be ranged along a continuum from those employing collective decision-making, including widespread discussion and consultation among staff, to total autocracy on the part of the head. Schools also varied in terms of the degree to which they saw their role(s) in the pilot scheme as merely an extension of what schools already do under conventional arrangements rather than as a major increase in their responsibilities. Finally, schools varied in the degree to which they saw good teaching as an indefinable art, and the degree to which they saw it in terms of definable and observable/measurable competencies.

Some issues

There was not unexpectedly a desire on the part of tutors to retain a degree of control in relation to school-based supervision. This was reflected in the following:

- earlier notification of selected schools would have been desirable;
- tutors needed to be clear about, and to have a common understanding of, the way in which schools were chosen;
- further clarification was needed of the role expectations and division of labour between tutors and schools/supervising teachers;
- some anxiety was expressed about the fact that school teacher supervisors may be less willing than college tutors to allow students to develop their own particular styles;
- tutors emphasized the importance of their traditional role through reporting that some schools were anxious about taking responsibility for students' progress, and especially at the prospect (should the scheme be extended to assessed practices) of having to judge a student to have failed.

At the end of the practice, tutors were generally positive about their experience of the pilot scheme, although a number of concerns, some of which confirmed anxieties expressed at the first meeting, were signalled:

- uncertainty about the precise role requirements of the tutor in the new scheme, with regard to (*inter alia*) precisely what to do on their visits and how these should be set up and conducted. Some uncertainty remained about this even at the end of the practice;
- schools' uncertainty about what was expected of them. For example, some were uncertain what they should do about unsatisfactory students, about student absences and attitudes, and about students' files;
- some teachers seemed to have unrealistic expectations of the students, and tutors wondered how, in these arrangements, this could be handled;
- negotiating access to the school, the teachers and the students was problematic. One school effectively 'shut out' the tutor to the point where she had to contact the students by telephone in order to check on their experience. Eventually, she insisted on her visit, but did not achieve this until the final week. This contrasted with other tutors who had negotiated access with ease or, in one case, simply informed the school when she would be visiting. What is clear is that the tutor's role was generally very much a negotiated one, not just in regard to access, but throughout the whole of the period.

Quality of supervision

Students' reports of the variation in teachers' attitudes were confirmed. These varied from highly directive supervision, where everything, from the setting out of lesson notes in the file through to the way finished work was to be displayed, was laid down by the school, to very laissez-faire approaches.

One tutor reported a student's concern that the class teacher was 'not objective enough' in the assessments she made, though this was an exception. Another, that teachers had sought feedback on their observation reports to students, that these had in general been less detailed than the ones he or she would have made, but that this was compensated for by the regular and on-going verbal feedback which the class teacher was able to give throughout the practice.

One tutor reported that one school had considered the 60/40 per cent time division was unrealistic, and there was considerable feeling that the one-hour formal supervision time was inappropriate. At least some teachers preferred to see the whole experience in a more 'organic' way, with the pattern of student experience negotiated with the student throughout, and the observations integrated into ongoing interaction.

Tutors confirmed that students appreciated working more closely and in a more continuous fashion with the class teacher, 'more as a colleague' than appeared to be the case where students were supervised by tutors in the traditional way. They confirmed that students generally felt they were receiving better support/ supervision/feedback than their peers in more conventional situations.

The tutors generally agreed that it would be desirable to allow schools/teachers considerable freedom to negotiate with the student the precise pattern of teaching/ non-teaching time and the way supervisory observations are organized in order to optimize integration.

Conclusion

There was agreement that:

- There is a need to make clear to schools that the role of the tutor, and therefore of the tutor's visits, are very different under arrangements like those of the pilot scheme.
- An early visit to the school is essential to assure students that they are on the right track, in respect of (*inter alia*) their files.
- Where difficulties were encountered on the practice, these were very often difficulties which occur also in more conventional arrangements.
- There is a tension (role-conflict) for teachers trying to be both supports/guides and assessors, and this may need resolution through using the college tutor, head teacher or another to undertake the assessment.

- Whether these arrangements place a greater burden of time on schools and their teachers is debatable; what is clear is that schools perceive the burden of responsibility to be greater. There was also some feeling that any scheme which involved more paperwork would be rejected by schools.
- The students believe the experience to be superior to that of conventional practices, and on balance this view was endorsed by the tutors.

Supervision as a shared experience

The above piece of research highlights the anxiety experienced by students when it comes to being the object of observation and assessment by those who seemingly wield power in relation to their transition to qualified teacher status. Of course, this situation has always existed and successful students have learned the techniques which enable the transition to proceed in a smooth manner. These constitute aspects of the *rites de passage* which are recognized by all who are involved in the process and, indeed, they are alluded to by Waite (1995) in an excellent ethnographic study of instructional supervision.

It would be reasonable to suppose that increased responsibility on the part of schools for the supervision of students on teaching practice would result in the 'upskilling' of those students. Prevailing wisdom suggests that teachers in schools who act as supervisors are in a better position to induct students into the practicalities of the classroom than university academics. Insofar as university tutors retain a role in this process, shared supervision might provide a measure of 'quality assurance' and this is surely a rational enough view of the attributes of the process. Yet, there is evidence (Waite, 1995, p. 24) that teachers and university tutors may collude in the maintenance of surface aspects of their role cultures. Proficiency in the technical skills of teaching may be then of less significance than the inculcation of an understanding of the 'culture' of teaching, that is, to know how 'to look and act like a teacher'. If this serves to challenge and undermine the official aims and objectives of bodies such as the Teacher Training Agency in England, or other accrediting or licensing bodies elsewhere, then it simply suggests that such bodies operate with a degree of naivety.

Chapter 4

Induction of Newly Qualified Teachers in Primary Schools

For many years there has been an awareness of the need for greater attention to the induction of new teachers and for meeting their needs during their initial placement in maintained schools. This chapter sets out to review the literature and discuss the key issues in the continuing training and education of new teachers during their first year in post, analysing the effectiveness of both formal and informal induction programmes, before making proposals for improving the process.

Too often experienced teachers speak about their own early experiences as being 'thrown in at the deep end' and left to sink or swim (Turner, 1982) or of 'hitting the ground running' (Thompson, 1993). Probation has not been a requirement since 1992 in schools in England and Wales, and Local Education Authorities (LEAs) have been concerned to ensure that newly qualified teachers have a properly supported first year. The abolition of the probationary year refocused attention on the need for properly planned and delivered induction in order to ensure quality control as well as the professional socialization, integration and retention of new teachers. In order to encourage development of schemes to meet these needs the government made available funds for joint LEA and Higher Education devised induction schemes through ring-fenced grants (such as Grants for Educational Support and Training – GEST).

Not all Local Authorities have provided well-organized schemes for supporting newly qualified teachers and not all schools are able to take advantage of the provision that has been made. Factors such as size of school, travelling distance from induction courses and the difficulties of finding supply cover to release new staff all make the induction and continuing professional development of newly qualified teachers problematic. (Some of the recommendations for improving the induction year experiences of new teachers at the end of this chapter may help schools who are coping with the problems caused by the withdrawal of regular probation support in schools by Local Education Authorities' advisory teachers following the abolition of the probationary year in 1992.)

History of the probation and induction of newly qualified teachers

It was in 1959 that the Minister of Education laid down the requirement for a teacher to undergo a probationary period of one year (Statutory Instrument 364, Regulation 19), in order to 'satisfy the Minister of his [*sic*] practical proficiency as a teacher', with the caveat that: 'During his probationary period a teacher shall be employed in such a school and under such supervision and conditions of work as shall be suitable to a teacher on probation.'

Some of the earliest indications of an awareness of the need for sensitive induction rather than the 'sink or swim' time of trial which that regulation suggested, appeared in an article by Bush (1966), who defined the first few years as the most critical period in a teaching career. Similar views on the need for nurturing individuals in organizations are to be found in works on management theory. Argyris (1964), writing on organizational theory, spoke of the need for a balance to be achieved between the need of individual employees to maintain self-esteem and the demands of the organization to achieve its ends of increasing outputs with decreasing inputs on a continuous basis. The Plowden Report (CACE, 1967) made it clear that there was a problem in teacher probation when it declared: 'It is doubtful if the majority of young teachers are given the conditions and guidance in their first posts which will reinforce their training and lead to rising standards in the profession as a whole' (para. 1000).

In the field of education, Owen (1968) was among the first to point to the need for a clearly planned programme of induction, when he asserted that 'the warm glow of undirected concern is no substitute for planned action, least of all in any attempt at innovation'. Taylor and Dale's 1971 major national survey of teachers in their first years of service (published 1973) revealed that only one in ten LEAs was running any scheme of induction guidance in 1966. This state of affairs led to the James Committee, looking at the education and training of teachers (DES, 1972a), making the statement: 'Nothing has impressed or depressed us more than the inadequacy of the present arrangements for the care of the probationers.' It recommended:

- that teacher education needs to be viewed as recurrent or cyclic throughout a teacher's professional life;
- that the school has a function in the education of teachers at all stages, in fact it should be seen as 'an essential part of its task' (James, para. 2.21);
- that the school's functions in in-service education are linked to the needs of planned change:

- that these functions will need co-ordinating by a professional tutor who will also act as a link with other agencies of teacher education.

The James report led to the White Paper *Education: A Framework for Expansion* (DES, 1972b), which set out recommendations for new teacher support in the probationary year: 'A teacher on first employment needs, and should be released part-time to profit from, a systematic programme of professional initiation, guided experience and further study ... "induction".' This led to the major DES-funded research project *The Teacher Induction Pilot Schemes* (Bolam, Baker and McMahon, 1979). In 1975, Bolam, in the middle of the TIPS research, stated publicly:

> Our evidence, and experience from earlier Bristol studies, led us to conclude that some probationers, teachers, Heads and Advisers were deeply cynical about the need for systematic induction on the scale envisaged in the James report. [There was a] prevalent definition of probation as a period of survival rather than of professional development. (Bolam, 1975a, p. 34)

In the same year, in the United States, Lortie published his pioneering work *Schoolteacher* (1975), in which he made the point that teaching seemed to be the only profession where the beginner becomes fully responsible from the first working day and performs the same task as a 25-year veteran, concluding: 'Compared with crafts, professions and highly skilled trades, arrangements for mediated entry are primitive in teaching.'

Maw (1975) argued a case for planned school-based induction led by a professional tutor who would also be responsible for ensuring ongoing professional development (on the James and White Paper pattern) for all teachers in the school, and Hammond (1976), reporting on conclusions of research in three West Country LEAs, proposed a pattern of induction support with 25 per cent release for new teachers and school-based professional tutors. It began to look as if in England and Wales the research findings and government concern about the placement, induction and retention of new teachers had been transformed into an official review of the situation. *Helping New Teachers* (DES, 1976) was published and this together with an experimental government-sponsored scheme (The Teacher Induction Pilot Scheme – TIPS, 1974–78), made it appear that the stage was set for government action for change. Baker (1977), in a review of LEAs which were active in providing induction, found that there was a move towards fulfilling the White Paper recommendations.

But in the end the issue was fudged. In 1977, following the National Conference on Teacher Induction at the University of Bristol, a Green Paper (Cmnd 6869) declared that the government had included in its envisaged financial provision increasing expenditure providing for release of teachers for in-service training and induction between 1977 and 1981. However, this was not so much an increase in funding to LEAs as advice as to how the same amount of money should be distributed. So, even granted that there was an acknowledged need and an administrative will, there was not the money to fund improved induction support for new teachers.

It was in response to this state of affairs that Norman Evans, in his book *Beginning Teaching in Professional Partnership* (1978), made the following comment on probation and induction:

> So this fifty year story ends with Government stating that induction during the first year is necessary, but there is very little money to support it. What induction will mean for new teachers is whatever can be devised within existing funds. (p. 15)

Despite the concern, the research, and even the Teacher Induction Pilot Schemes, it was clear that too little was being done too late to achieve the proposals of James and the 1972 White Paper – supportive induction for new teachers within the framework of ongoing staff development. In 1979 Zeichner published a major review, *Teacher Induction Practices in the United States and Great Britain*, which praised the aims of the Teacher Induction Pilot Scheme whilst regretting the reduction in the numbers of schemes and the paucity of induction elsewhere in the UK. He identified problems in implementation of induction as:

1. the expense of release;
2. the difficulty of getting suitable supply teachers to cover release;
3. the difficulty of releasing new teachers and mentors at the same time; and
4. the reluctance of mentors to observe new teachers and give them helpful feedback.

Overall he found reluctance in tutors to go beyond an advisory pastoral role into what he felt was a necessary active interventionist role. There was also a reluctance by practicing teachers to allow probationers to observe them. Zeichner found that new teachers felt that there was a tendency for LEA courses to replicate college work but that probationers enjoyed the peer group discussion they allowed. Zeichner recommended:

*   advisory committees on induction with wide representation;
*   the appointment and training of teacher tutors who should also work with initial teaching students on school placement;
*   induction courses should be evaluated by probationers on the basis of their direct practical relevance.

Citing Tisher (1979), Zeichner emphasized the reciprocal nature of induction and concluded that it must include ways of using the new knowledge and skills that neophytes bring to the profession.

Zeichner's research was followed up in Grant and Zeichner (1981) where it was shown that very few new teachers actually received any of the recommended benefits of job-embedded induction: just 19 per cent received any release time, 18 per cent had reduced class sizes, and only 10 per cent were exempted from non-classroom duties. Although 61 per cent received informal support from colleagues, this still meant that nearly half of the beginning teachers were being left to sink or swim. Grant felt that the need for induction had been shown in earlier research and emphasized that his findings revealed a continuing need for wider and more effective implementation.

McCabe and Woodward (1982), reviewing the success of some of the English teacher induction pilot schemes, especially in Northumberland, felt that there was not a great deal to show for the past decade's activity – particularly in terms of those relatively successful pilot schemes influencing the country as a whole. He felt that there was a greater consciousness of the need for induction in schools and that there was a need for the pilot LEAs to continue to attempt to influence other LEAs and schools and encourage them to undertake induction programmes.

In the same year, in the United States, Hall (1982) spoke of the need for more research into ways in which induction could be implemented and evaluated in order to be more effective. Wallace (1982) proposed that induction should be into the community as well as into the profession, suggesting that new teachers should be introduced to the people and businesses in the area around the school in order to achieve 'an eye witness view of the environments from which their students come'. Kevin Ryan, who had explored the experiences of new teachers in their first year in a New York school in *Biting the Apple* (1980), introduced his concept of 'the teachable moment' in 'Why Bother with Induction' (Ryan, 1982) – the idea that as new teachers face failure each day they are at their most ready to learn, and thus the need for induction to be available and of the right quality at the moment when new teachers are most psychologically disposed to learn is crucial for their success.

In the United Kingdom in 1982 Her Majesty's Inspectors' report *The New Teacher in School* was published with one of its key intentions:

> ii. to judge the extent to which schools make the best use of the skills, knowledge and training that new teachers bring to their first posts, and the extent to which support is provided where it is needed. (DES, 1982, p. 1)

The findings of the report showed some improvement over past surveys of induction but still found:

> three out of ten [probationers] are not being provided by the schools in which they have taken up their first post with conditions likely to promote their professional development and many of these are receiving little support from Heads or fellow staff. (p. 1)

Her Majesty's Inspectors found that in many cases new teachers who had problems had been poorly placed – in schools which did not match their training – and commented on how those who had best overcome this disadvantage had been well supported by the LEA and colleagues. Without an adequate support programme these new teachers had struggled and sometimes failed. As a result of these findings, amongst the HMIs' key recommendations were two on the importance of proper placement:

Those responsible for first appointments should take personal and temperamental factors into consideration as well as the academic and professional preparation of the candidates, in determining their fitness to teach in a particular school. (p. 81)

The appointment of teachers to schools should be the result of a thorough process of selection which seeks to ensure that the best possible match of qualifications and teaching tasks is achieved. This match is particularly important in the case of first posts, both in the interests of pupils and of the teachers themselves. (p. 82)

On the need for induction there is a more general statement that national guidelines should be set up (on the lines of the best practice they had seen and reported), 'to ensure both the acceptable minimum and the desirable levels of support that should be available for all new teachers both from the schools and the local authorities' (p. 82).

There is a suggestion that 'in the longer term' the probationary year should follow the induction year thus making it part of a two-year process (following the example of certain states in the USA). No further action has been taken on this, perhaps because the unions were astute enough to see it as a government attempt to reduce the pay of new teachers (giving them two years on an entry grade salary before they attained Main Professional Grade) and opposed it. (For a discussion of this issue see Reid, Bullough and Howarth, 1988.)

HMI (DES, 1982) again recommended that induction programmes should be drawn up bearing individual needs in mind, and they emphasized the particular needs of PGCE-trained teachers. Unfortunately there was no real funding available to support their recommendations and the report is prefaced with the caveat: 'Nothing in this discussion paper is to be construed as implying Government commitment to the provision of additional resources' (inside front cover).

There was much discussion in the press of the small percentage of teachers defined as below average in achievement (HMI defined it as 25 per cent but the schools had only found it to be 10 per cent). Malcolm Skilbeck, in an article in the *Times Educational Supplement* (5 November 1982), claimed that he was pleased that more than three-quarters of new teachers were doing so well but went on to say that the report revealed that:

a sufficiently large number of new entrants to teaching display such remediable deficiencies in their practical skills for us to accept two basic propositions: that more comprehensive and systematic probationary programmes are needed; and that pre-service training is capable of further improvement. (p. 4)

The wide-ranging publicity surrounding the publication of this report was to have little immediate effect – without an expansion of staffing and funding LEAs were unable to carry out the changes, however desirable they may have been. The DES responded to the suggestion that national guidelines should be laid down and in 1983 published Administrative Memorandum 1/83 entitled 'Assistance for probationers from school and LEA staff'. Despite these recommendations and the earlier advice that HMI and DES had published, Patrick, Bernbaum and Read (1984), in their research into the careers of PGCE-trained probationers, found that less than 30 per cent of their respondents were in schools which made any special arrangements to induct their new staff, and concluded: 'Despite the initiatives of the last twenty years a sizeable proportion of new teachers lacked opportunities to make the best use of their training and many of those in difficulties found no formal arrangement to offer them support' (p. 54). This view was reinforced in an Industrial Society publication, *Induction*, which looked at teachers in their first year of service (Trethowan and Smith, 1985) and in which it is stated: 'Induction is one of the great neglected areas of management in Great Britain ... There are few professions in which a member is considered fully trained as soon as he leaves College or University yet teaching comes close to this' (p. 2).

Andrews (1986), in his analysis of induction schemes in five countries, found that successful schemes had the following common characteristics:

1.   Beginning teachers receive reduced workload and release time.
2.   Beginning teachers, although not permanently certificated, receive a regular salary and obtain professional benefits, responsibilities and status.
3.   Beginning teachers are given opportunities to observe other teachers and to discuss their instructional and curricular practices.
4.   Professional induction seminars and workshops are regularly held for beginning teachers to meet and exchange ideas as well as to extend their professional knowledge and skill.
5.   Experienced teachers or mentors are assigned to work with beginning teachers and provide formative supervision. They receive a reduced workload.
6.   Principals or other assigned members of the beginning teacher's induction support team are responsible for providing summative evaluation and evaluative documentation on the progress and eventual recommendation of certification for the beginning teacher.
7.   In-service workshops are afforded members of the induction support team regarding supervision, communication, data gathering and counselling. (pp. 143–4)

In the mid 1980s there was a burgeoning of research interest in induction in the United States (where teacher shortages and teacher turnover were leading to problems of recruitment and retention of staff at the same time as there was a growing interest in staff development and quality assurance). See for instance Huling-Austin (1986), Varah et al. (1986), Stone (1987) and Rosenholtz (1989), who propose that it is the most able who are most likely to leave teaching in their early years and that only thorough induction support and on-going staff development will prevent escalation of the problem. Freshour and Hollmann (1990) went further in suggesting that assuring teacher retention by thorough induction not only saved money and problems (by avoiding advertisement and appointment expenses) but benefited the whole school by ensuring continuity and staff satisfaction.

In January/February of 1986, the *Journal of Teacher Education* devoted a special issue to teacher induction. Amongst the most detailed and trenchant of the papers in that issue is one by Fox and Singletary (1986) in which they begin by challenging the necessity of including the element of assessment into induction programmes – an element which they see as strikingly different to induction in other professions where the aim is solely to ease the transition from student to professional and where the success of the programme is adjudged rather than that of the individual. They propose four ingredients for a successful induction programme posited on its likelihood of increasing the retention of new teachers as productive and competent professionals:

  i. provision for acquiring additional knowledge and instructional skills;
  ii. opportunities for developing attitudes that foster effective teaching perform-ance;
  iii. assistance in recognizing the effects of isolation;
  iv. aid in becoming integrated into the school district and community. (p. 13)

Given that content, they then propose 'four reasonable goals' for effective induction seminars which they feel should:

1. Develop a psychological support system for the teacher, focusing on self perception and attitudes likely to result in increasing commitment and retention.
2. Assist in the development of acceptable models for solving problems that typically confront new teachers, especially methods of classroom management and discipline.
3. Help develop the skills necessary to transfer the pedagogic theories received in pre-service courses into appropriate teaching practices.
4. Provide experiences in which new teachers can begin to develop professional attitudes and the analytical and evaluative skills necessary to maintain a high level of proficiency in a continually changing profession. (p. 13)

By the mid 1980s the need for induction was largely accepted in the United States and there was a plethora of published criteria for induction programmes which sometimes made rather large claims for their efficacy. Huling-Austin (1986) responded with an article defining 'What Can and Cannot Reasonably Be Expected from Teacher Induction Programmes'. He suggested that such programmes can be expected:

1. To improve teaching performance.
2. To increase the retention of promising beginning teachers during the induction years ... And screen out the least promising if the program provides provision to do so.
3. To promote the personal and professional well-being of beginning teachers.
4. To satisfy the mandated requirements related to induction and certification.

On the other hand he asserts that induction programmes cannot reasonably be expected to:

- Overcome major problems in school context such as misplacements, overloads, overcrowded classes, etc.
- Develop into successful teachers those beginning teachers who enter the profession without the background, ability, and personal characteristics necessary to constitute the potential to be acceptable teachers.
- Substantially influence the long range retention of teachers in the profession if additional changes are not made in the educational system at large. (pp. 4–5)

8079
NC02422

In a report to the Canadian government on current practice and future options in teacher education, Fullan and Connelly (1987) suggested principles which should guide the construction of induction programmes:

- teacher education should be seen as developmental and lifelong;
- the responsibility for continuing teacher education should be shared between stakeholders;
- reform in teacher education can most meaningfully begin by attending to teachers new to the profession.

The pressure was also on administrators and principals in the United States to recruit and retain teachers, and Stone (1987) advised his fellow principals that the way to achieve this successfully was to implement effective induction programmes because they had the additional merit that 'If you succeed you may find yourself with an outstanding educator for years to come' (p. 35). Wilson and D'Arcy (1987), exploring the experiences of new teachers in Northern Ireland, found that the problem was not merely the provision of induction programmes but ensuring full participation (this insight is an enduring one and is highlighted in the most recent research). They found that teachers in the primary sector were at a double disadvantage by comparison with the secondary sector. Not only had they less time set aside for school-based induction activities but they were less able to participate in external courses which were designed to compensate for limited school provision. The authors thus concluded with the proposal that the probationary year for primary teachers should consist of a guaranteed teaching arrangement which included a properly developed induction programme.

In 1988, in the United States, Hunter produced a major review of the literature on teacher induction in which he concluded that the research revealed a clear need for induction programmes for beginning teachers during their first years in the profession. He found that the evidence was that new teachers who followed a programme of induction became better communicators, had superior working skills and made better progress in lesson preparation, handling class discussions and classroom management.

The same year brought the second version of *The New Teacher in School* (DES, 1988a), the report of a survey of HMI in England and Wales in 1987. Their findings on induction were that 'A substantial proportion of all schools were making no, or inadequate, provision for the needs of their new teachers' (p. 10). They went on to say that it was essential for LEAs and schools to appreciate that colleges could not prepare new teachers for every situation and therefore they must offer induction for all new teachers. In particular, HMI felt such aspects as 'working in open plan schools, liaising with parents and the community and carrying out pastoral and administrative duties should be included in induction programmes.'

Schools and probationers themselves felt that the support received fell short of what they were entitled to, so HMI reminded LEAs and schools that:

1.43 [they] should review their practice in the light of AM 1/83 to ensure that induction is effectively arranged and delivered.

1.44 At the very least all schools with newly trained teachers should have a plan for their induction and should make arrangements for the close monitoring of progress including the observation of, and feedback on, lessons taught ... There is a need for structured discussions between new teachers, even the most competent ones, and their senior colleagues to evaluate progress. In addition ... schools should devise ways in which pastoral staff can be more frequently involved in induction programmes.

1.45 Schools also need to consider carefully what special expertise new teachers have to offer and how this might best be used.

1.46 There is a need for closer liaison between schools and local authorities in defining their respective responsibilities for the induction of new teachers. The roles of local authority advisers need to be clarified and the extent of the support they can give to probationers defined realistically. All schools should have the benefit of written guidelines for induction from their local authorities. (p. 11)

Findings of recent research into induction

A major research project by Andrews (1987) revealed the variety of approaches to induction and staff development internationally and pointed to the need for clearly planned and executed induction as part of a 'confluence' of the three aspects of teacher education – initial, induction and in-service.

Five Induction Paradigms (Andrews, 1987)

Induction paradigms	General characteristics
1. Laissez-faire	• absence of formal programming • minimal mentor–protégé relationships • not a high priority for beginning teachers or staff-development programming
2. Collegial	• informal supervisory relationship with experienced colleague • in-service activities are provided for both participants • no assessment component enters into this supervisory relationship
3. Formalized mentor-protégé	• formalized contractual relationship of beginning teacher with experienced teacher with mandated syllabus • comprehensive in-service activities for both participants • beginning teacher evolves through a continuum from dependence on the mentor to professional independence

	• an assessment component is part of the mentor's role
4. Mandatory competence-based	• mandated competency-based performance programme • probationary status of beginning teacher emphasized • major financial and legislative support provided • well monitored and evaluated
5. self-directing professional	• self directed contract format • may combine elements of paradigms 2, 3 and 4 • mentor provides collaborative support • beginning of on-going professional development plan

Her Majesty's Inspectors' (1988) findings in relation to the primary sector were that:

- in 93 per cent of primary schools expectations of new teachers were high or too high;
- in about 40 per cent of primary schools good or adequate provision was made for the induction of new staff;
- in more than 30 per cent less than adequate or no provision was being made;
- most new teachers were receiving good or adequate support from their heads;
- other members of staff were supportive to the great majority;
- more than 50 per cent received less than adequate support from their LEAs;
- about 30 per cent received insufficient advice on lesson preparation;
- more than half received insufficient advice on lesson evaluation;
- 30 per cent felt that they needed more advice on classroom organization;
- about a third would have liked more advice on pastoral care.

Predictably, the reactions that this major government publication caused included much policy drafting and committee creation within LEAs, but actual change was slower. This makes it all the more poignant that Reid, Bullock and Howarth (1988), after reviewing past and present literature on probation and induction, ended with the assertion: 'How a new teacher starts is likely to determine much more than initial success – it is likely to shape his entire career' (p. 171).

Tickle (1989), in an article on probation as a preparation for professionalism, reported that there was little evidence in recent research of actual improvements in induction despite much rhetoric about the need for improvement. Quaglia (1989) came to a similar conclusion: 'Current school policies and organizational practices do not adequately ease the transition of beginning teachers into the educational profession' (p. 7). In 1993 the Office for Standards in Education produced a report entitled *The New Teacher in School 1992* based on the latest survey of induction by HMI. The conclusions echoed earlier reports but revealed some development in provision. Notably they revealed:

> Three quarters of primary heads indicated that an induction programme had been planned although the new teachers judged much of this provision to have been minimal.

> A significant weakness of induction programmes was that they did not build on initial teacher training experiences in any significant manner. Schools were largely unaware of the strengths and weaknesses or of the previous teaching experiences of new teachers at the end of their initial training.

> Induction was largely dependent upon the new teachers identifying their own needs. It was unusual for objectives and outcomes to have been jointly agreed between the teacher, the school and the LEA.

> Priority in induction was rarely given to pedagogical or curriculum needs. Most schools saw their role as one of support rather than of training. Personal support, however, was often good and was much appreciated by the new teachers.

> Induction rarely compensated for shortcomings in initial training. Some weaknesses were common to both the induction period and ITT.

> Most LEAs planned an induction programme but provision was very varied and not always well targeted. Liaison between LEAs and schools in respect of induction was poor. Visits by LEA staff were welcomed and judged by the new teachers to be helpful.

> School support was of critical importance for weak teachers. A high proportion of such teachers experienced poor induction. This was often linked to schools which had a higher than average number of difficulties. Too often the schools were unaware of the nature of the weaknesses which were consequently not remedied.

> About 10% of the new teachers in this survey were considered by HMI to be ill-suited to teaching. (p. 38)

Earley's 1992 NFER survey of teacher induction in schools (which he defined as 'the process enabling new teachers to become effective') came up with similar findings to the HMI on matters of fact, but was exclusively based on an analysis of 72 LEAs' responses to questionnaires and thus does not consider the viewpoint of the NQTs. Significant areas of agreement and difference (with my commentary interpolated) were: 'Nearly two fifths of LEAs and schools provided funds for pre-appointment visits, whilst one fifth funded pre-appointment LEA visits and introductions' (p. ii). Thus three-fifths of NQTs did not get pre-appointment visits to their schools and four-fifths did not have visits to meet LEA officers and facilities – most new teachers had to pick up details of their workplace and employers as they taught a full timetable. 'All LEAs arranged a central (and/or area based) induction programme and three quarters saw this as an important incentive' (p. ii). At a time when there was a shortage of primary teachers some LEAs saw induction pro-grammes as part of their recruitment package rather than as central to a policy of continuing professional development. 'There was considerable variation between LEAs in the number of days each new teacher was entitled to follow an induction programme' (p. ii).

Far from accepting the earlier James Report or DES suggestions about one-tenth release time for NQTs, the majority of LEAs (56 per cent) managed to fund six days or less per year, and often this came out of the school's total allowance for staff development. One-tenth of a new teacher's timetable would be 42 days – the failure to achieve the recommendations of the James Report, TIPS research and earlier government publications is revealed by the fact that only 6 per cent of LEAs released NQTs for induction for twenty days or more.

Earley's correspondents felt that LEA centre-based courses were 'cost effective inputs and were able to take a broader perspective than would be possible within an individual school' (p. iii). (However, because very few primary schools were able to run school-based induction courses, new teachers were not getting the balancing contextually based development they often required.)

Local Education Authorities who responded to Earley's survey made it clear that they did not have close links with higher education institutions who provided ITT, and that they were not generally concerned to build links for the provision of induction. Some made an exception in order to gain GEST funding for induction development programmes and to gain HE accreditation of LEA-run induction courses. The LEAs identified that the key areas of teacher competence which they found to be inadequately covered by initial training were classroom organization and management and the management of pupil behaviour and discipline.

The LEAs saw their most important work for the future of induction to be in the development and training of mentors who would deliver programmes of support for NQTs within their own schools. Most of Earley's respondents in this survey spoke of their concern for the future of induction programmes under new government funding arrangements and expressed concern that new teachers should have an entitlement to 'at least a minimum amount of induction training and support' (Earley, 1992, p. v).

My own research (Turner, 1992) looked at the approaches to the management of induction employed by five Local Education Authorities in England. An analysis of their policies on and implementation of induction support employing a model adapted from Andrews (1987) made it clear that there had been recent developments in the way in which these were managed. There was a tension between two developmental tendencies: some were moving towards a *status-maintained (historical)* model in which new teachers' support programmes had developed from a 'laissez-faire' approach towards a legislation-based, centrally controlled pathway which was concerned with measuring competency and ensuring quality. Others were moving from laissez-faire towards *individualized professional development*, an idealized theoretical model, more concerned with setting up collegial support and with encouraging the self-developing professional. It became clear in 1995 that there was a decision from government – via the Teacher Training Agency – to provide a clearly legislated pathway of broad range of entry approaches to teacher training controlled by a pattern of competences. This was driven by a concern to achieve a common standard of teacher quality by introducing an exit profile based on the achievement of the competences. Thus a status-maintained centralist model has been introduced with the public intention of encouraging individual continuing professional development.

Relationships emerged as an important factor in the effectiveness of the implementation of induction, particularly those between the new teachers and LEA inspectors and advisers. Where pleasant, helpful and non-judgemental support and advice was given, in situations where relationships were good and status differentials did not interfere, new teachers' self-esteem and performance were improved. These good relationships were more apparent in the LEAs which were moving towards *individualized professional development*.

School-based induction

The next stage of analysis was of the effectiveness of the management of induction in individual schools. I found that differences between schools within particular LEAs were as great as differences between LEAs in many cases, but that schools which had explicit plans for induction programmes and which were consistent in carrying out those plans were most likely to enable their new teachers to have a successful first year. One new teacher who benefited from a well-planned and consistently delivered induction programme said:

> I feel happy about the way my induction has gone. I've had a great deal of support from the staff in and out of school. I've been luckier than most probationers I've spoken to – I get a lot of willing help.

In contrast another, very able, new teacher who did not get a consistent induction programme, complained: 'Nobody has seen me teach from the school. Record books are the only contact. I'm not getting any comments or feedback. [Induction is] not being managed or monitored. I'm not supported.'

The role of head teachers was pivotal in the management of probation support and induction programmes and in the supervision of designated teacher mentors. This reinforces the finding that where relationships were sympathetic and supportive new teachers felt more comfortable and able to co-operate and contribute – where relationships were formal and judgemental there was a tendency for new teachers to keep their heads down, conform and survive rather than develop individual strengths. One NQT whose head teacher was very formal and distant commented on a progress report he had been shown:

> The comments were mainly satisfactory. It's disappointing that he hasn't been in [to

observe teaching] and I can't see how he can judge. He occasionally pops in with a message and leaves immediately. He seems to judge me on what he sees in passing.

In another school where the head teacher was clearly supportive a new teacher commented:

The head had us in to chat to us at the end of last term and then he handed us our reports and asked us for comments – I was very happy. He was very positive and felt that I fitted in well and worked hard.

Another factor in new teachers' relative success was the extent of relevant school-based induction and its match to individual needs. New teachers, their mentors and head teachers all spoke of the effectiveness of the school-based element of induction – even though it fell short of the James Report recommendations of 20 per cent timetable release or even the DES' later 10 per cent – and of the importance of more resources being made available to increase it.

Really they need more released time for training and support – at least five days over the year. (Head K)

Probationers come in with lots of good ideas. They need time to look around and see how others do things and time to reflect, prepare and evaluate in school time. (Mentor H)

I think if you are talking about releasing them from class responsibility ... one third of a day per week would be absolutely ideal – to let them go and observe other people, to let them do a bit of extra preparation and to get the feeling that they're a bit special and that people are making special provision for them. (Advisory Head E)

If self-developing, reflective professionals of the kind suggested by the Individualized professional development model are going to be encouraged they will need an individualized, contextually relevant induction programme (with a clear school-based emphasis) linking their initial training with future INSET.

Placement was a significant factor in new teacher success. New teachers needed appropriate school placement – which matched their training and teaching practice experience as well as their preferred age range, if they were to approach their first teaching post with confidence. Where the new teacher was appropriately placed, with a supportive head teacher, had an empathetic mentor and showed signs of being self-aware and reflective they made good progress, but where a teacher was placed in a school with one or more of these factors absent there was a likelihood of their being less successful. Critical exceptions included 'Tanya', who maintained a high standard of success despite lack of support from head teacher and mentor because she was very able, internalized her locus of control and used appropriate social strategies, and 'Keiran' who had a non-supportive mentor, lacked self-awareness and reflectiveness but survived because he was appropriately placed with a determined and supportive head teacher.

One interesting finding was that in some schools where two new teachers were placed there were major differences between them in terms of success and development. These differences were examined by the creation of detailed case studies on those individuals. The interview data was analysed in terms of the new teachers' awareness of their own strengths and weaknesses and their attitude to criticism and advice (using a version of Lacey's teacher socialization strategies) and this was compared with the views expressed by their head teachers, mentors and visiting advisory teachers. The resulting analysis was compared with the factors governing 'locus of control' (Kremer-Hayon, 1987, adapted from Rotter, 1966). This examines the way in which people locate the reasons for their success or failure: internally – in such a way as to accept their own role in controlling the world, or externally – in which they see success and failure as caused by outside factors.

As socialization is one of the key factors in individual adjustment to the role of professional in an organization I have also used Lacey's (1977) concepts of 'social strategies' (adapted from Becker et al., 1961) to examine the way in which individuals have faced up to, adapted to or struggled with the situations in which they have found themselves in their probationary year. These three varieties of situational adjustment Lacey describes thus:

1. *Strategic compliance*, in which the individual complies with the authority figure's definition of the situation and the constraints of the situation but retains private reservations about them.
2. *Internalized adjustment*, in which the individual complies with the constraints and believes that the constraints of the situation are for the best.
3. *Strategic redefinition*, [in which] they achieve change by causing or enabling those with formal power to change their interpretation of what is happening in the situation. (Lacey, 1977, pp. 72–3, my emphasis)

In applying Lacey's terminology to my case studies I use a similar adaptation to that suggested by Zeichner and Tabachnick (1985) and Etheridge (1989), by including successful and unsuccessful versions of some of the social strategies, when I suggest that Keiran hovers between unsuccessful internalized adjustment and unsuccessful strategic redefinition.

I also introduce into the analysis the concept of internal–external locus of control (Rotter, 1966) as adapted by Kremer-Hayon (1987). I utilize the key descriptors – as listed below – rather than applying the Locus of Control Scale when applying the concept to my case studies. Kremer-Hayon adapts Phares (1976) to establish the key characteristics of externally oriented teachers and internally oriented teachers (in terms of their definitions of the locus of power).

Externally oriented teachers:
- depend more heavily on outer resources;
- tend to conform relatively easily to social norms (Phares, 1976);
- are not active in efforts to shape their environment;
- possess less perceptual sensitivity (Phares, 1976);
- are less willing to correct personal shortcomings;

- do not perceive various teaching tasks as being difficult;
- are more dependent on authority and people ranking higher in the professional hierarchy [for evaluation]. (Kremer-Hayon, 1987, p. 31)

By contrast let us look at internally oriented teachers (here I extrapolate rather than directly quote).

Internally oriented teachers:
- depend on their own resources;
- sometimes find difficulty in conforming;
- actively set out to shape their environment to fit their own style;
- show perceptual sensitivity;
- are willing to correct personal shortcomings;
- perceive difficulties in planning, implementation and discipline;
- are less dependent on 'higher authority' for evaluation.

It was Kremer-Hayon's conclusion however that so clearly struck a chord with my own findings:

> The fact that externally oriented teachers do not tend to perceive difficulties in their classroom teaching may lead to some illusions on their part and in turn a perceived lack of the need to improve. The more internally oriented teachers probably need some support to help them alleviate the difficulties they perceive. (p. 32)

The resulting analysis revealed a pattern in which those new teachers with an internalized locus of control (who recognized their own responsibility for their actions), and with social strategies of internalized adjustment or strategic redefinition, were most able to cope with the stresses of their first year in teaching and move on to become strong teachers. Where new teachers had an externalized locus of control (and saw the reasons for their lack of success or slow progress as residing entirely outside of themselves), if they also employed the social strategy of strategic redefinition, they were likely to be unsuccessful as teachers. If they employed the social strategy of strategic compliance and were supported by their mentors and schools they tended to survive and gradually adapt to their roles.

More recently, Pomeroy (1993), in a survey of all English higher education teacher training institutions, examined the way in which both pre-service and induction training of new teachers has relied on school-based mentors whose training has varied enormously both in its content and quality. A detailed critique of a variety of aspects of mentoring and induction in initial and ongoing school-based teacher training has been offered by Smith and West-Burnham (1993). Wilkin and Sankey (1994) have examined the ways in which the increasingly school-based teacher education brought about by Department for Education (DFE) Administrative Memoranda 9/92 and 14/93 are employing a range of approaches to mentor training and support within partnership approaches to training and induction for beginning teachers.

The balance between school-based and LEA centre-based induction

This is one of the key dilemmas facing induction course planners – well-planned, appropriate and individually focused induction schemes delivered by committed heads or teacher tutors in schools meet the needs of most probationers and solve problems of cost of transport and replacement teachers. On the other hand the LEA needs to induct teachers into its philosophy, systems and resources, and some schools are not willing or able to design and deliver effective school-based induction so it is the LEAs' responsibility. A third aspect of the problem is that whilst it is difficult for LEAs to meet the needs of all new teachers, and courses are therefore pitched at the average expectation, in their own schools probationers rarely get the opportunity to meet, discuss and share problems and successes with other new teachers.

Local Authorities in England and Wales are gradually having to become more and more entrepreneurial and competitive, and schools are receiving more of the money from GEST funding for in-service training, including induction of new teachers. This market economy will impinge on the quantity and quality of induction support received. Perhaps before making recommendations about ways in which funding and time can best be shared between LEA and school-based induction, it is worth looking at the findings of research.

The research in this area classically reflects the dilemmas we have been discussing. Hammond (1976) argued for greater balance between LEA and school-based programmes for new teachers and suggested that connections with inductees' colleges should be established. The classic dilemma for the new teacher has always been wanting to be treated as 'a real teacher' whilst at the same time needing support and information from others. Lortie (1975) noted that new teachers wanted limited interference in their classrooms from their superiors but at the same time wanted their superiors to act as buffers between them and bureaucracy, parents and difficult students. Maw (1975) looked at the induction needs of new teachers and emphasized that they should be seen as part of any ongoing school-based in-service programmes but that the school should be aware of providing them with individual support. New teachers he felt should be recognized as needing special training to meet their individual needs but not conceptualized as 'learner/novice' in comparison to the rest of the staff who saw themselves as 'experienced/experts'.

Baker (1977) argued that schools can do a lot to help new teachers and that in a period of financial constraint:

> the reduction of teaching loads for probationers may be difficult to establish and LEA schemes without it may be seriously weakened, since release of the probationers is an essential component in facilitating the induction process. Nevertheless, the induction of probationers still remains a task for schools at present and much can be done within the school even without a large-scale, expensive LEA scheme. (p. 64)

Baker (1977) goes on to argue, in his conclusion, for the central importance of a teacher tutor, and claims that 'the teacher tutor role can be successfully created and integrated into the school systems as part of the school's support system for probationers' (p. 74). In concluding, Baker argues that teacher tutors should in future add counselling and supervision skills to their repertoire rather than confining themselves to a pastoral role and that their training skills should be employed by the school as part of its ongoing staff development policy for all staff.

These views were powerfully echoed by McCabe (1978) in a paper on the problems of the probationary year, in which he concluded: 'To have any chance of being effective, induction, or any other inservice work, must be in a very real sense school based, probably with someone like a teacher tutor in charge of it' (p. 144). McCabe came to these conclusions because he found LEA policy was not being effectively achieved – often the only action taken was to circulate a letter on induction policy to heads and to follow up with a telephone call if it became apparent that the policy was not being carried out.

Bolam, Baker and McMahon (1979) saw the LEAs' most important function as monitoring and evaluating:

> Advisers should concentrate on clarifying, supporting and evaluating school based induction programmes and the tutor's role through discussion with heads and teachers in individual schools rather than on running and participating in external courses for probationers. (section 12.9)

One LEA that followed this advice was Barnet. Dawkins (1979) reported that Barnet allowed half-day release each week for new teachers and that their induction was focused on school-based activities designed to meet the individual needs of the new teachers led by LEA-trained teacher tutors. Centre-based sessions were more general and were run by advisers. The ILEA followed a similar policy when it advised in its 1980 report on induction of probationers that the school-organized component was the most important to be achieved and that key elements were the release time for probationers for observation and visits to other schools. Similarly, Newcastle, researched by Smyth and McCabe (1980), achieved continuing success in induction through co-operation between heads and teacher tutors on school-based courses and a limited centre-based component. Smyth and McCabe go on to say that probationers missed the opportunities to meet other new teachers and to go on visits to other schools because of the reduced LEA budget for external courses.

Sadly, despite the importance given to school-based induction and support, McMahon (1981) found that only 49 per cent of LEAs produced an induction handbook for new teachers or chose to write out their policy. McMahon declared that very few schools knew their LEA's policy on induction. In the same paper, McMahon reported that although 43 per cent of LEAs made specific recommendations about how to organize school-based induction, they rarely evaluated its level of uptake or success. These conclusions were supported by the DES report on the

HMI survey of induction. *The New Teacher in School* (1982) found that many new teachers received little or no support from their head teachers and that many schools had no induction programme at all.

Tisher (1982) undertook international research into the needs of new teachers and came up with a list of essential elements for school-based induction:

1. experienced teachers as induction/professional development tutors;
2. special training for tutors before they began induction;
3. a detailed programme for school-based induction which recognised teacher collaboration and the new teacher's creative involvement. (p. 104)

After 1982, perhaps inspired by the DES report, many LEAs began to expand the centre-based aspect of their induction programmes, but Hutchinson (1982) was amongst the critics who pointed out that new teachers were more concerned with the practical solution of classroom-based problems in their schools, and saw LEA external courses as nothing more than an escape and a respite.

The best summary of the development of the relationship between school-based and centre-based induction support is from Bolam (1984), and is largely based on the findings of the Teacher Induction Pilot Schemes. Bolam argues that external courses:

> however good, were necessarily general and thus peripheral to the probationers' major professional concerns which were to do with their particular pupils, classrooms and schools. Probationers' main source of practical help lay in the school, with colleagues and the headteacher. (p. 2470)

Bolam found that attendance at centre-based courses was less than enthusiastic, with 77 per cent attending day-release courses (some had release problems) and 39 per cent on average attending optional evening sessions, and summarized:

> Probationers consistently said that they wanted practical help with their specific practical problems but they gave considerable support for the course as an opportunity to meet and talk with other probationers; the therapeutic value of such external courses should not be underestimated ... [However] lectures and informal individual discussions were over-used by tutors compared with what the probationers wanted, whereas workshops, films, case study material and group discussions were underused. (p. 2470)

The problem of assessment and evaluation is never far from the minds of new teachers, and it was for this reason that Fox and Singletary (1986) recommended that LEA external induction courses should not be run by inspectors and advisers (who carried with them their evaluative function) but by teachers' centre wardens or university staff.

Reid, Bullock and Howarth (1988) came down on the side of school-based bias to induction in their research findings, and declared:

> There is increasing evidence that courses which are school based; are run by 'internal' rather than 'external' staff; include probationers who are being 'fostered' by teacher tutors [with] positive personalities and attitudes towards their work, stand the greatest chance of success. (p. 165)

Despite the growth of more sophisticated centre-based courses and more concern by LEAs to sell themselves to new teachers as employers, the research (both in the United States and the United Kingdom) continues to come down heavily in favour of a bigger proportion of induction being carried out in schools. Heath-Camp and Camp (1990) recommend a school-based induction programme for all new teachers which begins with a thorough orientation – spread over time to allow absorption – and includes an 'Everything you need to know' handbook as well as in-service training and staff development spread over the first year. Similar recommendations are made by Cole (1990), who proposes school-based induction programmes with the following elements:

1. professional development or induction teams;
2. school-based orientation programmes;
3. new teacher handbooks;
4. peer coaching and mentoring handbooks;
5. peer support groups;
6. special professional development sessions;
7. classroom observation opportunities.

Cole (1990) concludes: 'Perhaps the most important step towards helping teachers become real [sic] involves preparing a school context that is conducive to growth not endurance and that welcomes new teachers and helps them to develop as enquiring professionals' (p. 104).

So it can be seen that over time and across national boundaries there has grown up a realization that induction, to be effective, needs to be essentially school-based and to be managed by a professional tutor, as well as giving opportunities for peer discussion and for observation both outside and within the school. Any LEA induction should be clearly focused on philosophy, policies and resources.

Teacher and tutor release for induction

In order that induction can be effectively organized and realized there is a need for both the new teacher and his or her tutor to have time, both individually and mutually, released from other school duties to plan, prepare, observe, evaluate, inform and discuss. A brief review of the research reveals a continuing concern that this should be maximized, and awareness that insufficient priority for release time has been given by governments and local authorities and schools. The James Report (1972) recommended that new teachers should be released for 30 days for induction training in their first year. Conners and Jennings (1975) recommended that new teachers should be released from their classes in order to be able to have time for 'essential preparation'. Hammond (1976) went further than James in his recommendation that new teachers should only have 75 per cent timetable with the remainder of time devoted to induction and preparation, and the TIPS research (Bolam, 1977) reinforced this view when it suggested 60 days release for new teachers in their first year. Sellars and Crowther (1977) took a similar view, asserting that probationers were unused to extended periods of teaching, and the associated preparation and the stress connected with the socialization process made their situation even worse – for these reasons he argued new teachers both needed and appreciated a reduced teaching load.

Unfortunately LEAs and schools were not always able to provide the release time to make induction effective. Davis (1980), reviewing the Liverpool induction scheme – in which heads were asked to provide release for tutors and probationers and were given the necessary resources – found too often that release time was not granted because heads felt 'constrained by other priorities'. The situation was worse elsewhere in the UK – McMahon and Bolam (1981) in their survey of LEA induction schemes reported: 'Unfortunately very few authorities are providing release time' (p. 7). They went on to reveal that less than 20 per cent of their sample of 104 LEAs had granted any release time for induction. Of these, two allowed a day per week, twelve half a day a week and the rest less time.

Recognizing that release for induction training was important – and not happening – the DES referred to it in *Teaching Quality* (1983b), where they said: 'It is particularly during the probationary period that new teachers should be given reduced teaching loads and other appropriate support' (para. 85). The report goes on to make it clear that it is the LEA's duty to provide for in-service training, including induction, from within present funding (which the DES intended to 'maintain at least at current levels').

In the United States, Fox and Singletary (1986) proposed that school districts should co-operate with schools in allowing release time for new teachers to attend induction seminars in order to alleviate the difficulties of new teachers having to attend so many meetings out of school and also to demonstrate their belief in the importance of induction. Jesse Goodman (1987) supported that view and went on to claim that new teachers needed release time to plan for curriculum development and working jointly with their teacher tutors to 'conceptualize and develop unique curricula and strategies for instruction'. In this way Goodman claimed schools could help novices develop into proactive and reflective practitioners.

The second DES publication entitled *The New Teacher in School* (1988a) does not quantify release time but declares that the most effective schools 'provided for probationers' needs by giving them a lightened workload' (p. 63), whilst admitting that nearly half of their sample (42 per cent) provided poorly or not at all for the needs of probationers.

Crawley (1990) mixed good news with bad on the problems of release time for probationers. Her account of the effective use of the half a day per week release granted by the ILEA concludes with the news that in the restructured London boroughs less time and fewer resources are available for induction than before.

In summary, then, release is seen as a key factor in the effective achievement of an induction programme – both school based and external centre based – and both the new teacher and the teacher tutor need release time individually and mutually if its effectiveness is to be maximized. New teachers need time to prepare, evaluate, observe others, visit other schools and attend courses; their tutors need time for their own training, to observe, discuss issues, evaluate and deliver training. The use of release time – structured and supervised, or not, is less urgent as a debate when so little is available. On balance it appears that new teachers need a proportion of it for their own immediate purposes, but some at least should be structured and aimed towards longer-term development targets.

Recent LEA responses to improving induction

Since 1992 Local Education Authorities have been encouraged to work with schools and higher education institutions to set up partnership approaches to induction and to bid for government Grants for Education Support and Training (GEST) funding for these schemes. In the next section of the chapter we describe in some detail the setting up of one LEA's Partnership Professional Portfolio Induction schemes and its link with competency profiling. The structure and activities of the steering committee and working party are outlined. The development of the professional portfolio, its contents and presentation, its trialling, and its marketing to the schools is described. An evaluation research project into its effectiveness carried out by the four universities is described and discussed. The sample, methodology, questioning technique and the methods of analysis are described and critically examined. The detailed results of the research are listed, together with some recommendations for improving the operation of the induction year and the presentation of the portfolio. The relationship between HEIs and the LEA in induction year development and mentor training is examined. The way in which the universities collaborated to ensure that those teachers who wished could register for accreditation on presentation of a portfolio which evaluated their year's work and progress in a reflective manner is described. University support for the mentoring programme and the production of working materials is outlined.

LEA/HE partnership in induction

LEA G's scheme for Induction and Professional Development has been a classic example of the ways in which government Grants for Educational Support and Training (GEST) have enabled innovative projects. In response to the government's decision to abolish the probationary year and to encourage local authorities to improve induction for newly qualified teachers, the county council set up a partnership group with four universities. These universities, Anglia Polytechnic

University; Homerton College, Cambridge; University of Brighton and the University of Greenwich, agreed to work together with the LEA Development and Advisory Service to devise a professional portfolio to support newly qualified teachers in their induction year. The working party was led by a seconded deputy head and included teacher representatives from both primary and secondary schools. Administrative Memorandum 2/92 suggested LEAs should improve the connections between themselves and colleges and departments of education in the transfer of newly qualified teachers from college to their first posts. To that end, the DFE proposed the development of exit profiles which would inform the induction year and subsequent professional development through INSET. This was the lever by which the DFE, following the pressure from central government and the Department for Employment, pushed profiles of competences onto the LEAs – because that was one of the conditions which they had to meet to gain GEST funding.

The partnership working party set out to list the competences they would expect of newly qualified teachers, (a) for secondary teachers, and (b) for primary teachers. These lists pre-dated the DFE 9/92 and 14/93 lists of competences but were not significantly different.

The Professional Development Portfolio was a successful and innovative project employing the expertise of heads, advisers, mentors, NQTs and representatives from four universities. The materials were designed to provide the widest possible range of support for mentors and NQTs and perhaps suffered from being too bulky and daunting in the earlier versions.

A research project was set up to evaluate the materials and has had a clear influence on the more user-friendly materials which were issued in 1995. Despite the best efforts of the LEA team it became clear that not all schools, heads, mentors and NQTs were using the materials. Many who had obtained the portfolios but did not attend the LEA mentoring and induction courses were not sure how to use them.

There is still a clear need to put the induction programme and professional portfolio structures more fully in place by:

1. early delivery of the materials for use by heads, mentors and NQTs – preferably in the term before NQTs begin their jobs;
2. enhancing the use of the portfolios by mentors and NQTs by ensuring the materials are widely understood within schools and that mentors receive training in their use by attending the training courses;
3. enabling NQTs to benefit not only from support and pastoral care but also from professional development derived from the critical reflection and training provided by well-trained mentors;
4. continuing evaluation by the LEA of the implementation of the materials, and the training courses for mentors;

5. matching induction and subsequent staff development for NQTs to individual needs.

Since the research was completed, the LEA has already addressed all five of the recommendations outlined above and has implemented many of the points made in the paper.

Recommendations for improving the induction of primary teachers

There are fourteen key issues and consequent recommendations, the first six of which centre on human relationships, and the remaining eight of which are concerned with organizational matters. Initial school placement revealed itself to be a key factor which influenced both affective and organizational elements and is therefore discussed as a connecting element between the two sections.

The role of the individual – human relationship factors

1. Research confirms the central role of the head teacher in induction of new teachers – as pivotal manager, gatekeeper of time and resources, agenda setter, and model for (and important influence on) relationships and staff attitudes within the school.

   New teachers come to their first placement wanting to feel like 'real teachers' and to be recognized as such, at the same time as needing much advice and support in order to achieve classroom success. For this to be fulfilled head teachers need to be sensitive and aware in their dealings with new teachers and to designate responsible teachers to act as mentors to them (in order to avoid the confusion between assessment and guidance which can shadow heads' relationships with new teachers).

   This suggests that primary head teachers themselves need training, advice and support (in terms of time and resources) in order to be able to fulfil their essential part in induction of new staff.

2. New teachers emphasized the significance of the role of the advisory teacher in managing LEA provision of supervision, assessment and advice for new teachers – especially their ability to create non-threatening and supportive relationships at the same time as providing purposeful training. As outsiders to the school – with an LEA-wide view of the new teacher's situation – they were able to be both a sympathetic ear and a provider of a broad perspective (able to tell the new teachers that they were well off in their schools or recognize the difficulty of their placement and support them appropriately).

   Wherever possible advisory teachers or other mentors independent of the school should provide continuity between LEA and other outside courses and school-based inputs. They could also design complementary training for those who need particular support.

3. The evidence derived from interviews in the schools suggests that there is a key role for teacher mentors in the induction process in schools which has not yet been fully realized or exploited. The evidence from many of the managers in the process suggested that the provision of mentors with supportive and sympathetic personal-ities delivering structured programmes could be the key to a much improved induction process. These mentors have to be capable of forming good relationships with the new teachers – personal as well as professional – in order to become 'buddy' as well as trainer and assessor if they are to be effective. Head teachers, as responsible managers, need to monitor both the induction programme and the mentor–trainee relationships to ensure success. The key to these relationships is mutual respect – with heads, mentors and colleagues treating new teachers as respected colleagues with worthwhile knowledge and skills to offer but in need of initial support in order to fit in with the school and establish themselves in the classroom. There was also evidence to suggest that, given sufficient training and enough release time to become actively involved in support and training, the mentor's role in induction could become central to continuing professional devel-opment and school improvement.

Mentors should be carefully chosen and trained in all aspects of their roles. They should be given sufficient status in the school to bring about the necessary changes in support and training for NQTs and colleagues, and monitored by their line manager to ensure that their input and relationships are successful.

4. Many new teachers and head teachers emphasized the importance of recogniz-ing, valuing and making effective use of the knowledge and skills that new teachers bring to the school as an aspect of induction and professional socialization.

Heads and mentors should actively promote the specialized knowledge and individual skills trainees bring with them, both for the self-esteem of the trainees and for the good of the school as a community.

5. Case studies of newly qualified teachers have examined the effect of personal cognitive style (particularly locus of control) and social strategies employed on the success of new teachers in schools. They have suggested that able and confident individuals who have an internalized locus of control, combined with the social strategy of strategic redefinition (or strategic compliance), tended to be the most successful in their induction year.

Heads and mentors need to work with trainees to enable them accurately to assess their relative success and failure – providing support and training where needed and putting overly harsh self-criticism into context. Frank discussion of the individual's role in fitting in to the needs of the organization and in contributing to its development will help new teachers to become socialized into their role as teachers.

The linking factor

6. The importance of appropriate placement of new teachers in their first school has been identified by many researchers and commentators. New teachers perform best when their placement is relevant to their training in terms of age-range and philosophy and relevant to their teaching practice experiences. Where there has been an unavoidable inappropriate placement it needs to be accompanied by sympathetic induction and mentoring which is supported and monitored by the head teacher. It is clear that where new teachers are placed in schools which fit their training and age-range preference they have fewer initial problems. Where they share the school philosophy it is most likely that their induction and socialization struggle (efforts to become a competent teacher and full member of staff) will be met with empathy and practical help.

New teachers need to be placed in a school where they can cope in their induction year. This means due consideration needs to be given to their age-range specialism and subject specialism in training and to their previous experiences as a trainee teacher. It also means that they need to be placed in a room which is near to their mentor and/or other supporting teacher rather than in an outside portable classroom by themselves. With the increase of LMS and GM schools, the LEA has less and less to do with appointment and it will be a school's job to ensure that the candidate's experiences and qualifications are appropriate for them to undergo induction in their school.

The role of organizations – policy and management factors

7. Examples of well-organized school-based induction policies and programmes (written, timetabled and clearly managed) were not common in any of the research. My research revealed a relationship between NQT success in the induction year and well-planned and consistently carried out induction policies.

It would be worthwhile for schools to put in place structured induction programmes for NQTs (OFSTED inspections will probably hasten this process). Also important is an extension of the time available for meeting the immediate classroom and school training needs of new teachers and giving a greater priority to school-based induction.

8. The importance of release time being made available to new teachers and their mentors (separately and occasionally jointly) to enable the induction programme to be effective has been one of the most frequent conclusions of all the research. Since the introduction of directed time, some teachers felt that if they were not given time to do the job they were unable to do it. The most effective schools found ways to release both mentors and NQTs, often using staff development and GEST budgets.

If both mentors and new teachers are to be able to observe, discuss and reflect individually and jointly, time needs to be put aside to release them. There is evidence that where this happens both parties report increased effectiveness in their teaching and increased job satisfaction.

9. Learning by observation, reflection, feedback and target-setting is central to the government's approach to improving teaching quality. There is still a professional reluctance to intrude on other teachers' classrooms and evidence that it was still not happening in many schools (DES and OFSTED reports, *The New Teacher in School* 1982, 1988a and 1993). Most of my respondents reinforced the need for all new teachers to be observed teaching by mentors and/or head teachers. It was felt that they needed to be seen teaching and to get feedback in order to allay their fears about progress and/or to provide the necessary advice on making improvements in practice sufficient for them to achieve QT status. There was clear criticism from a minority of NQTs of mentors and head teachers who made judgements on their progress as teachers without observing lessons. New teachers were also critical of head teachers, mentors and advisers who expected trainees to know how they were getting on without giving feedback based on observation.

Regular planned and structured observation with clear feedback and encouragement of reflection is a necessary part of a new teacher's development. Jointly agreed targets should be set for the next development period with training and examples of good practice provided to enable the desired improvement.

10. The opportunity to observe other appropriate teachers working was a highly valued learning experience for most of the new teachers interviewed and some felt they had too few opportunities. Equally, the opportunity to visit and observe in other appropriate schools as part of their induction was not usually available although most new teachers mentioned this as an important learning experience which they would like to have included in induction.

Because the induction year is the time when new teachers come to terms with what they still need to know about teaching, the opportunity to observe experienced and skilful teachers in a range of different contexts provides a most stimulating and important input to their learning.

11. There was clear evidence in most of the surveys of induction that the role of the mentor (or designated teacher) was not well established in most schools and was often seen and felt to be a low status role (mainly a 'buddy' role or a pastoral role). Some head teachers and mentors felt that the role should be extended to include training and that mentors could become staff development tutors in order to raise their status, ensure the ongoing training of all teachers and provide a career route.

Making mentors more clearly part of the school management team and giving them status among the staff would help to improve the impact they have on staff development and school improvement. As mentoring in school-based teacher training and school improvement programmes become more common it is clear that the mentor could take on the role of staff development officer or master teacher and be central to management of the institution.

12. The research revealed the importance of LEAs getting their administrative procedures for probation and induction working effectively, for these policies to be clearly communicated to all stakeholders and for systems to be evaluated to ensure they were working efficiently. Many interviewees also felt that it was the job of the LEA to ensure that there were effective working relationships among all those involved in the process. Increasingly, LEAs have an almost impossible job as more schools become independent of them via LMS and GM processes. They are required to set up policy and provide services which schools do not have to accept. It is clear that LEAs need to offer the right balance of activities with a range of choices available for schools and individual trainees to select from. There is a danger that the pressure to provide a single economical course of induction frustrates the schools' and inductees' particular needs and that these clients, offered all-or-nothing programmes, too often opt for the latter.

LEAs should offer a menu of short courses and training options for mentors and newly qualified teachers which allows them to complement school-based training and to select according to their individual needs and the exigencies of their school budget.

13. Most interviewees wanted changes in LEA centre-based induction courses in order that they would (a) deliver information, techniques and ideas in the most effective order for new teachers; (b) attempt to meet more effectively the individual needs of new teachers (e.g. infant, junior or secondary; B.Ed. or PGCE; trained in England and Wales or overseas); (c) complement more effectively initial training and ongoing school-based teacher development.

Many of the demands of schools, mentors and newly qualified teachers are now being met by the provision of distance learning packages and menus of in-service courses. Nevertheless, many teachers still complain that LEA course titles are ambiguous and the content repetitive – sharper attention to the needs of clients will enable LEAs to maintain a role in induction.

14. Many interviewees in management posts (head teachers, advisers and inspectors) spoke of the importance of seeing teacher education as an ongoing process and of wanting to build more effective links between stages of teacher education. They felt that there should be clearer links between initial teacher training institutions, LEAs and schools involved in induction programmes. Equally many respondents saw the need for further connection between school-based staff development, in-service provision and higher education courses – ensuring broader teacher involvement and giving credit for courses attended.

School-based teacher training is leading to changes in mentor training, initial teacher training course delivery by teachers and in higher education involvement in schools. The connections between induction and mentoring, and the accreditation of teachers' INSET, are leading to the creation of continuous professional development portfolios for teachers. Recent government publications have suggested the need for teachers to demonstrate continuing professional development as part of their appraisal process and perhaps in future (as in medicine, law and engineering) as a necessary part of retaining professional status.

Conclusion

The interaction between organizations in the management of probation and induction is too complex to admit a simple conclusion. Human relationships and attitudes have the greatest effect and the head teacher is the most significant figure in the web of relationships. Differences between LEAs' policies and implementation are less significant, and even the differences in quantity and quality of school-based induction do not have such a major effect on new teacher development.

The best placement for newly qualified teachers in their induction year is in a school which is appropriately matched to their training (both in age-range, specialism and in philosophy) and which has a caring and pastoral management run by people who both support and respect the inductee whilst allowing them to develop their own teaching style and encouraging them to share their particular expertise.

Where the human relationships are well handled, new teachers are enabled to develop as reflective and contributing fellow professionals despite such serious difficulties as inappropriate placement, inadequate organization and poor resources. Where induction is not well managed, the less resilient new teachers leave their school, their LEA or even leave teaching altogether – a tragic waste of their self-esteem, training and expertise and of the long-term stability and reputation of the profession.

The United States has been in this situation before us and sudden changes in teacher supply, linked with poorly managed induction and professional development, have sorely affected their teacher retention. Houston and Felder (1982) offer useful advice which is still relevant:

> When a new teacher becomes frustrated, anxiety ridden and exhausted, the students and the entire profession suffer. New teachers must be inducted into the profession humanely, in ways that engender pride, openness and increased professional competence and stature. (p. 460)

Chapter 5

Induction of Newly Qualified Teachers in Secondary Schools

The general introduction to the history of induction has been covered in some depth in the previous chapter and the same recommendations and principles apply. At the simple human level, helping new colleagues to make the transition from student to teacher not only reflects favourably on the personnel management and pastoral resources of the institution in which they are placed but builds collegiality and loyalty. The evidence from the United States is that careful induction helps retain the new teachers in their posts for longer than was usual (Huling-Austin, 1986; Varah et al., 1986; Freshour and Holman, 1990). Secondary schools in the UK have always had a high turnover of new staff but the evidence seems to be that schools which provide good induction programmes (perhaps as one element of an Investors in People policy) will not only retain staff but will have a head start in improving school standards through the resulting stability and commitment of the staff.

But there are other reasons for ensuring that new teachers benefit from induction. It has long been recognized that Initial Teacher Training has been unable to meet the needs of all teachers in all situations. Although the 1988 Education Act and subsequent National Curriculum have imposed a new orthodoxy on what is studied in schools, each school is still very different and new teachers need to learn how their school works and what their precise role will be within it. Subject departments and faculties are organized in different ways and new colleagues, especially newly qualified teachers, need to be introduced not only to school and department structures and procedures but to the less official level of 'how we do things here'.

Within their specialist subject or subjects newly qualified teachers (NQTs) will need to be clearly informed about the particular approaches, syllabuses, textbooks and methodologies which are used within the department(s) they will work in. More problematically, they need to know much of this well before they begin to teach. Curriculum and timetable information needs to reach NQTs in time for them to ascertain that they are sufficiently knowledgeable to teach these things, or, alternatively, that they need to read up and prepare materials in particular areas.

It is never sufficient, however, only to send new teachers all the necessary documentation. Most of us would receive school documents gratefully and attempt to read them before starting teaching but often they are not transparent to outside readers. Because all schools are unique, they also have their own 'ideolect' or particular use of language (jargon, if you like) and they also refer to people, roles, places and procedures which are known to the writer but unknown to the reader. What new colleagues need is a brief 'Introduction to X School' and 'Introduction to the Practical Sciences Faculty' and perhaps 'The Geography Department'. But more than that they need the opportunity to go through key points in the handbooks with their head of department and/or mentor. The material of the handbooks would be a useful part of the ongoing induction and mentoring programmes offered to all new colleagues.

Recent books on the subject contain many lists of what induction should include (I include several of these in the references at the end of this chapter). Clearly these are constantly in need of evaluation and review. The latest government publication on the subject, AM 2/92, makes the following suggestions:

Assistance for NQTs
8. Before taking up appointment:
i.   the opportunity to meet the head teacher, the head of department where appropriate and fellow members of staff;
ii. information from the school in the form of a staff handbook ...
iii. adequate notice of the timetable to be taught;
iv. all curricular documents, including statutory documents relating to the National Curriculum, relevant to the subjects he or she will teach;
v.   information about equipment and other resources available for use, including information technology;
vi. information about support and supervision provided by the school, and, in the case of LEA maintained schools, any additional support provided by the LEA.

9.   After taking up appointment the NQT should be able, so far as is practicable:
i.   to seek help and guidance from a nominated member of staff who has been adequately prepared for the role, and from the head of department, where appropriate;
ii. to observe experienced colleagues teaching;
iii. to visit and observe teaching in other schools;
iv. to become aware of the role of their school in the local community;
v.   to have some of their teaching observed by experienced colleagues and/or LEA advisers; to receive prompt written as well as oral feedback on the teaching observed; and to receive advice as necessary;
vi. to have regular discussions and opportunities to share experiences with other NQTs; and
vii. in the case of teachers in LEA maintained schools, to attend any meetings of NQTs organized by the LEA.

The document goes on to say that LEA induction programmes 'should complement not duplicate provision by schools' and that LEAs should ensure that all NQTs in schools maintained by them should be 'known and adequately supported'.

Most schools now have a sound base of documentation – staff handbooks, induction handbooks etc. (as required for Office of Standards in Education inspections) – but often knowledge of all of the documentation is restricted to senior management and information is not always updated to take into account recent legislation, policy changes within the school and curriculum development. One way to keep changes recorded without having to withdraw current handbooks is for a senior manager to keep the handbooks in both computer and looseleaf file form in order that an updated handbook can be produced for new colleagues at any time (existing colleagues would have had updated information circulated on a regular basis).

Induction and Continuing Professional Development

One role of induction is to be the next stage in the teacher's continuing professional education. The new teacher's professional profile from the university, together with the Teacher Training Agency 'Career Entry Profile', will increasingly inform the agenda for more individualized induction programmes. The need for clearer individual elements to induction courses has been pointed to in the literature (e.g. OFSTED, 1993a, DES 2/92).

The New Teacher in School (OFSTED, 1993b) reports newly qualified teachers as saying that they are not well prepared: to use IT in their teaching; to develop pupils' ability to communicate effectively; or to manage effectively the pace of lessons. Many reported that they felt poorly prepared to assess pupils' work and record and report on pupil progress.

Although there has been increased attention to these topics in university courses since first the Committee for the Accreditation of Teacher Education and then OFSTED with its Framework for Teacher Education highlighted them, there is still a clear need for these and other significant gaps to be addressed. This can best be done during induction and as part of the teacher's ongoing professional development because in many cases the school context is significant in the achievement of these aspects of teaching competence.

It is worth noting that those NQTs who felt unable to focus on assessment and recording in their first two terms reported that it was because of the 'crowdedness' of their experience of full-time teaching, but they were clear that they wanted to focus on it as an aspect of their professional development from the end of their first year into their second year.

If we are to aim to improve the teaching profession the easiest place to begin is with new teachers both by welcoming them to the profession and by setting up procedures whereby continuing professional development, based on self-reflection as well as peer and management assessment of needs, becomes established as a norm. Engineers, lawyers and doctors have established codes of practice concerning updating and renewal of professional expertise which many teachers would aspire to. (This is one of the aims of the emergent but not yet officially accepted General Teachers Council.) There is certainly great interest in this concept in the profession. Recent postgraduate research topics by teachers on in-service courses in universities have increasingly focused on such topics as 'The role of the mentor in continuing professional development', 'Peer appraisal in staff development', 'Head teacher mentoring', 'Peer mentoring for staff development and school improvement' and 'Profiling induction and continuous professional development'.

Balance between school-delivered and LEA-delivered programmes

Secondary schools, because they are large organizations, have a more structured approach to staff management and development, including induction. Most large secondary schools appoint a deputy head or senior teacher to act as professional tutor responsible for co-operating with HEIs on placement and school-based training of student teachers, acting as leader of induction programmes and often in charge of staff development. Most of the actual mentoring in secondary schools is undertaken by subject teachers (often heads of department) according to OFSTED (1993b) and Earley and Kinder (1994). Subsequently the great majority of secondary schools offer induction programmes to their newly qualified teachers which are jointly run by the professional development tutor and the heads of department. Most Local Education Authorities have schemes to which schools can send their NQTs (with facilities for grant maintained schools to buy in). In some cases these schemes are detailed, long-term, profile-based (see, for example, the Essex scheme, the Surrey scheme and the Devon scheme for induction). In most cases these induction schemes are now linked to higher education, and successful completion of the year's programme carries with it credit points towards in-service postgraduate qualifications. (These are generally called Credit Accumulation and Transfer Schemes and allow teachers to accumulate points towards awards such as advanced diplomas and masters degrees. Most universities recognize these points which are thus transferable if the teacher wishes to change the HE institution at which they are registered for an award.)

How effectively are induction programmes delivered?

One key problem which is identified in OFSTED 1993b and echoed in much of the other literature on induction (e.g. Turner, 1993 and 1994a; Hogben and Lawson, 1984; Huffman and Leak, 1986; Tickle, 1994) is the unwillingness of mentors to teach or train new teachers. 'Most schools saw their role as one of support rather than of training. Personal support, however, was often good and was appreciated by the new teachers' (OFSTED, 1993b, p. 38).

It is easy to see the receding locus of responsibility so common in school pupils' education ('Didn't they teach you that at infant school ... junior school ... in the lower school ... at O level?' etc.) repeating itself in professional education. There is an element of demarcation here: 'It's not my job to teach them how to teach – the university should have done that – but as a colleague I'll happily show them the ropes in the school.' This, combined with the tradition of non-interference in other teachers' classrooms, can lead to a situation where easily identifiable problems of new teachers with simple solutions are nevertheless not identified and solved because it would be seen as unprofessional or 'Not my job'.

It is to be hoped that the clearer identification of newly qualified teachers' competences, strengths and developmental needs which university profiling and the OFSTED Career Entry Profile will provide, will lead to agendas for individual induction programmes. At the same time, improved mentor training by higher education and Local Authorities will help to signal that training and development are part of the school's job and that the mentor is the key agent in the process.

What is surprising, twenty years on from the Teacher Induction Pilot Schemes research (Bolam, 1975), is that many NQTs still report that they have not been observed teaching (DFE, 1992; OFSTED, 1993b). Recent research with secondary NQTs revealed that half of them (44 out of 89) had not been observed by November of their induction year (Tickle, 1994, p. 188). The idea that new teachers should be observed and given feedback is reinforced in the literature and the legislation of the last 37 years. This was first recommended in Ministry of Education SI 364 (1959) and most recently restated in DFE Administrative Memorandum 2/92:

> 9. After taking up appointment the NQT should be able, so far as is practicable ...
> v. to have some of their teaching observed by experienced colleagues and/or LEA advisers; to receive prompt written as well as oral feedback on the teaching observed; and to receive advice as necessary. (Annex A)

This DFE memorandum, *Induction of New Teachers*, also points to the need to:

- improve links between initial teacher training, induction of NQTs and INSET during the early years of teachers' careers, particularly through the development of profiling and competence-based approaches to professional development;
- improve co-ordination between the induction activities of LEAs and those of schools;

- encourage provision which is carefully differentiated to meet the particular needs of individual teachers and groups of teachers who will have obtained qualified teacher status through a variety of different routes;
- help to ensure that those responsible for induction training are effectively prepared for this role;
- help to improve the quality of written guidance and other materials used in the induction of NQTs. (p. 2)

There has been a consistent awareness of what new teachers need in order to develop and how it can be achieved. The TIPS research (Bolam, 1975a), mentioned above, recommended that new teachers be given a reduced timetable (75 per cent of normal teaching load), 60 days release for induction training, trained teacher tutors or mentors to work alongside them and a school-based induction programme which included:

(a) An expenses-paid pre-service visit
(b) An intensive orientation period in September
(c) Regular, systematic discussion of lesson plans and pupils' work with a 'tutor'/experienced colleague
(d) Regular, systematic observation of the probationer's teaching with a 'tutor'/experienced colleague
(e) Regular, systematic observation by the probationers of a 'tutor'/experienced colleague teaching
(f) Regular structured probationer discussion groups
(g) Visits to other schools
(h) Systematic observation of the probationer's teaching, possibly by someone other than the teacher tutor, on three occasions (once a term) as part of the formal probationary year assessment process. (p. 12.4, section 3)

However, one does not need to look far to find the reasons for these recommendations not being universally implemented. Although these are principles which the government has approved there has been little money made available to enable Local Education Authorities or schools to achieve them. *The New Teacher in School 1992* (OFSTED, 1993b) survey by Her Majesty's Inspectors makes the point that many new teachers are not getting sufficient induction support and training. Although NQTs were usually given a lighter timetable, 'additional non-contact time was rarely used for induction. Only in a minority of cases was some of the time used for meetings with senior staff as part of a structured programme' (p. 35, para. 5.8). Even the recent GEST funding earmarked for induction following the publication of Administrative Memorandum 2/92, *The Induction of Teachers*, was insufficient to meet the recommendations of early researchers such as Lord James and Bolam et al.'s TIPS report.

It was, however, this earmarked GEST funding which led to much research and development from local authorities (e.g. Essex, Surrey and Oxford) in the area of induction and resulted in the provision of a series of training courses for mentors and newly qualified teachers, as well as the production of supporting packages of materials for future support. These packages became necessary because local authorities were no longer able to provide new teachers with the support of inspectors and advisory teachers on a full basis. This had happened because of the transfer of funding to schools via the Local Management of Schools reforms and the direct payment of government funds for induction and in-service funding to the schools themselves. However, some secondary schools feel that they want to induct their own staff because there are problems of inappropriateness, repetition and lack of complementariness in LEA courses (Maude and Turner, 1993).

Another reason for the necessity of induction support was the scrapping of the probationary year for new teachers. Although the government's logical arguments for this were concerned with the lack of effectiveness of the process in 'getting rid of weak teachers' they actually resulted in weakening the support and training process for improving teachers' competences in their first year because local authorities were no longer responsible for the monitoring of probationary teachers' progress.

Earley and Kinder (*Initiation Rights*, 1993) were told by secondary schools that all newly qualified teachers were being observed teaching in their schools (admittedly sometimes on an informal 'popping-in' basis) and that where there were difficulties this observation would become more formalized and regular. In contrast, HMI reported (OFSTED, 1993b) that in many cases the teachers with difficulties turned out not to have received regular observation, feedback and support:

> A quarter of the unsatisfactory teachers were in difficult schools ... The quality of induction training in these schools was often unsatisfactory. In many cases the new teachers' weaknesses had not been identified. They lacked models of good practice to draw upon and were unable to obtain suitable professional advice to improve their own practice. (p. 37, para. 5.19)

Perhaps the most encouraging factor in recent approaches to induction has been the growth of staff development programmes in secondary schools with senior managers as Staff Development Officers. These programmes have usually included induction as the first stage of staff development, and subsequently job descriptions, policies and procedures have been set in place to ensure that induction is carried out effectively.

In many cases these schools have come to terms with the need for professional tutors and mentors through being involved in articled and licensed teacher schemes. Their experience of the benefits for staff in training others has led them to set up schemes which embrace teacher trainees (often on a variety of courses and from different universities) under a common core provision. This provision has been extended for newly qualified teachers – in some cases to cover a two-year programme – and those teachers who have gained experience with teacher training often become mentors to NQTs in their induction year.

Recent legislation and its effect on teacher induction

Government Administrative Memorandum 9/92 and OFSTED's (1993a) 'Blue Paper', *The Government's Proposals for the Reform of Initial Teacher Training*, spelled out some of the ways in which the training of teachers was to change. Because these changes affect the whole pattern of teacher training, induction and continuing professional development it is worth reviewing them here before examining in detail how they have influenced induction for secondary teachers.

Circular 9/92 recommended that schools be given a much more important role in the recruitment, training and assessment of new teachers. The circular envisaged teachers playing a leading role in the design and delivery of courses for new teachers using their specialist knowledge and their experience of the immediate needs of teachers in secondary schools.

New teachers were expected to spend a much greater proportion of their training in schools – 24 weeks out of the normal 36-week PGCE course because, the Blue Paper states, 'The best way to learn classroom skills needed for effective teaching is by observing and working with teachers, as well as by discussing classroom practice with teachers, tutors and other students' (p. 4, para. 8). Circular 9/92 required all courses to equip new teachers with a set of 'competences' which included subject knowledge and personal and professional skills necessary to manage, maintain order and teach effectively in their classrooms. Most importantly, for the area we are examining, the Blue Paper states that, 'The development of complete profiles of new teachers' competences will ease the transition from initial training to induction' (p. 4, para. 8).

This concern with the profiling of competence acting as a structure for linking the three phases of teacher education – initial training, induction and in-service professional development – is one of the two key concepts we need to take from 9/92 and the Blue Paper. The other is the development of partnerships between higher education institutions (essentially the universities' departments of education) and secondary schools.

The development of consortia of schools to deliver secondary Post Graduate Certificates in Education has been one of the success stories of the 1990s, despite much resistance from many schools, the education establishment in universities and the teacher unions. A few independent school-centred initial teacher training consortia have been set up – notably the Chiltern group, the Anglian Coastal consortium, The Chelmer Valley consortium and the Bromley group. However, most of the new partnerships are adaptations of existing school/university arrangements teaching essentially the same courses in much the same way. Teachers, however, have greater involvement in direct supervision of students and of the content of their subject and education studies.

Anglia Polytechnic University, which had not at that point been running a secondary PGCE but had secondary expertise through shortened B.Ed. courses and licensed teacher routeways, decided to accept the challenge of 9/92 and invite secondary schools to become partners with them in designing and running a completely new course which would meet the new criteria. The first meetings with schools were totally unlike other course development meetings – we began with a transparency of the school year and imposed on that the university pattern. The key questions we asked the heads and senior teachers were:

- When do you feel it would be best for these trainee teachers to be in your schools: (a) for the best learning opportunities; and (b) to best fit in with school opportunities and difficulties?
- How should the pattern of placements be organized? Should there be blocks of time in schools or should there be continuous practice in schools on a two or three day a week basis or would a mixture of both best serve the students and schools?
- How many schools should trainees be placed in and how should they be chosen and counter-balanced?
- What roles should teachers play in the design and delivery of the course, and how would the schools and the university interact over assessment of both practical teaching and the academic aspects of the course?

The answers that this development group (four schools in the Thurrock area of Essex) came up with were radical and challenging. They felt that trainees should belong to their school and thus be treated as members of staff rather than visitors because they would spend 18 of their 24 school-based weeks in their home school. The second school – ideally selected to offer a contrasting experience – would be an opportunity to compare and contrast what had been learned in their home school and would offer a five-week experience. There was a clear decision that the second experience should be a real teaching practice offering training opportunities and a contrast of experience in order that a second view of the student's future suitability could be obtained, rather than just a visit to see how another school worked. One week would be set aside for a brief experience in a primary school in order for trainees to gain an overview of the whole process of schooling and more specifically to understand where their pupils were coming from in curricular knowledge.

The first real problem for schools was to decide when it was best for the students to be in schools in order best to learn their profession. Initially the decision was made that students should be in schools for the first two weeks of the autumn term because that is when classes were set up and organized for the year – thus the best time to witness class management, discipline and administrative procedures being applied. Schools did not want students in during the examination periods because it would not be a useful time for them to observe teaching and because teachers always felt under stress at those times. There was some debate over whether there would be any point in students being in schools during the last two weeks of the autumn term because of the timetable disturbance caused by Christmas events –

with some insisting that this would be an experience of what schools are really like, whilst others felt it would be a waste of time. Interestingly, after the first year, teachers decided they did not want the students in during the first two weeks of term because they wanted people in who knew what to observe, who had some inkling of the National Curriculum and who could begin to understand how to plan a lesson. Eventually students spent about half of the autumn term in schools on either intermittent or full-time experiences, all of the spring term in schools (with half-term week back at the university) and their final teaching experience was the first half of the summer term.

These schools embraced the government's suggestion that schools should play a larger role in the selection of teacher education students and arranged that interviews should be school-based. They insisted potential trainees should spend the morning in classrooms with teacher and children in order that classroom teachers could have an input about their potential suitability before the interviews. Each consortium of schools agreed that they would share the interviewing, with each subject being managed by one school but with each school having a right to send a representative to the interviews. The university subject representatives were also invited to each series of interviews and were asked to chair the panel which distributed students to first and second schools once the cohort had been selected (thus avoiding any unfair advantage accruing to the interviewing school). The criteria for placement were that the student would best fit into a particular department, that there should be a complementariness between the school A and school B placements and that the travel arrangements were possible for students.

The steering group of head teachers was clearly committed to the idea of ownership in the course and to the concept of partnership embracing all aspects of the new secondary PGCE. Thus each aspect of the course planning was carried out by delegated groups which consisted of one teacher from each of the consortium schools and one university representative. The teachers had a clear majority and made the major decisions at each stage of the planning process, with the university providing a steer on the 9/92 regulations and university procedures. The process was begun by the English team, and the resulting pattern of course planning was used by the other subject groups in order that there was a common format for the course document. It was decided that teachers would play a key role in the delivery of every part of the course, both in school and at the university, and that the university would deliver some of the work in schools. Both teachers and university tutors would be involved in assessment, with the exception of teaching practice, which would be totally assessed and evaluated by teachers, with the university offering a monitoring and moderating overview.

The course would be validated by the university and managed by a university course manager but the decision-making processes on course management, assessment and evaluation would be managed by the teacher-dominated course committee. The course was to be a partnership between the consortium of schools and the university, and teachers were to play a major role in all aspects of recruitment, selection, course design, assessment and evaluation.

Induction, mentoring and staff development were central to the scheme, with teachers receiving five days of university input on the course and their role in teaching the students in schools as mentors or professional tutors. An early element of the course was concerned with ensuring that the new students were effectively inducted into their host schools. The course was delivered jointly by senior teachers and university staff, and teachers who completed the course and submitted an assignment were eligible to register for credit towards further educational qualifications through the university. The university provided a link tutor who organized regular meetings of mentors and professional tutors in order to monitor the progress of the students and to evaluate and design the mentoring courses.

The mentoring began by ensuring that all mentors and professional tutors were knowledgeable about course documents and procedures, including assignments, assessment and reports. Other key elements concerned the skills of observing, note-making and giving verbal and written feedback. The mentoring course also covered aspects of recent government legislation which affect the PGCE, time management, counselling and tutoring, teaching adults and planning for continuing professional development. Teachers who registered for credits towards further qualifications were offered tutorials on their assignments.

A Short Bibliography on Mentors, Mentoring and Induction

Acton, R., Kirkham, G. and Smith, P. (1992) *Mentoring: A Core Skills Pack*. Crewe and Alsager College.

Booth, M. (1993) 'The effectiveness and role of the mentor in school: the students' view.' *Cambridge Journal of Education*, **23**(2).

Booth, M., Furlong, J. and Wilkin, M. (eds) (1990) *Partnership in Initial Teacher Training*. London: Cassell.

Daloz, L. (1986) *Effective Teaching and Mentoring: Realizing the Transformational Power of Adult Learning*. San Francisco: Jossey-Bass.

Department of Education and Science (1982) *The New Teacher in School*. London: HMSO.

Department of Education and Science (1988a) *The New Teacher in School*. London: HMSO.

Department of Education and Science (1988b) *The Education Reform Act*. London: HMSO.

Earley, P. and Kinder, K. (1994) *Initiation Rights: Effective Induction Practices for New Teachers*. Slough: National Foundation for Educational Research.

Earley, P. and Kinder, K. (1992) *Beyond Initial Teacher Training: Induction and the Role of the LEA*. Slough: National Foundation for Educational Research.

Eraut, M. (1985) 'Knowledge creation and knowledge use in professional contexts.' *Studies in Higher Education*, **10**(2).

Field, B. and Field, T. (eds) (1994) *Teachers as Mentors: A Practical Guide*. London: Falmer Press.

Fish, D. (1989) *Learning Through Practice in Initial Teacher Education*. London: Kogan Page.

Fox, S.M. and Singletary, T. (1986) 'Deductions about supportive induction.' *Journal of Teacher Education*, **37**(1).

Furlong, J., Maynard, M., Miles, S. and Wilkin, M. (1994) *Secondary Active Mentoring Programme*. Cambridge: Pearson Publishing.

Furlong, J. and Maynard, T. (1995) *Mentoring Student Teachers: The Growth of Professional Knowledge*. London and New York: Routledge.

Furlong, V., Hirst, P., Pocklington, K. and Miles, S. (1988) *Initial Teacher Training and the Role of the Schools*. Buckingham: Open University Press.

Hagger, H., Burn, K., and McIntyre, D. (1995) *The School Mentor Handbook: Essential Skills and Strategies for Working with Student Teachers*. London: Kogan Page.

Jaworski, B. (1993) *Mentoring in Mathematics Teaching*. London: Falmer Press.

Jennings, S. (1994) *Introduction to Mentoring in Teacher Education*. Exeter: University of Exeter.

Kerry, T. and Mayes, A.S. (eds) (1995) *Issues in Mentoring*. London and New York: Routledge for Open University.

Kremer-Hayon, L. (1987) 'Perceived teaching difficulties of beginning teachers.' *Research in Education*, **37**.

Lacey, C. (1977) *The Socialisation of Teachers*. London: Methuen.

McIntyre, D., Hagger, H. and Wilkin, M. (eds) (1993) *Mentoring: Perspectives on School-based Teacher Education*. London: Kogan Page.

Moon, B. and Mayes, A.S. (1994) *Teaching and Learning in the Secondary School*. London: Routledge.

Nias, J. (1984) 'Learning and acting the roles: in school support for primary teachers.' *Educational Review*, **36**(1).

Nias, J. (1989) *Primary Teachers Talking: A Study of School as Work*. London: Routledge.

OFSTED (1993) *The New Teacher in School 1992*. London: HMSO.

Quaglia, R. (1989) 'Socialization of the beginning teacher: a theoretical model from the empirical literature.' *Research in Rural Education*, **5**(3).

Reid, I., Constable, H. and Griffiths, R. (1995) *Teacher Education Reform*. London: Paul Chapman.

Shaw, R. (1992) *Teacher Training in Secondary Schools*. London: Kogan Page.

Smith, P. and West-Burnham, J. (1993) *Mentoring in the Effective School*. Harlow: Longman.

Stephens, P. (1996) *Essential Mentoring Skills: A Practical Handbook for School-based Teacher Educators*. Cheltenham: Stanley Thornes.

Tickle, L. (1994) *The Induction of New Teachers: Reflective Professional Practice*. London: Cassell.

Tomlinson, P. (1995) *Understanding Mentoring: Reflective Strategies for School-based Teacher Preparation*. Buckingham: Open University Press.

Turner, M.A. (1982) 'The deep end.' *Times Educational Supplement*, No. 3461, 29 November.

Turner, M.A. (1983) *Problems of Teachers of English in their Probationary Year* (Occasional Research Paper No. 7). Brentwood, Chelmer Institute of Higher Education.

Turner, M.A. (1992) 'The management of the probation and induction of teachers in primary schools.' University of Sussex D.Phil. thesis, (Unpublished).

Turner, M.A. (1993) 'The complementary roles of the headteacher, the mentor and the advisory teacher in school-based teacher training.' *Mentoring*, **1**(2).

Turner, M.A. (1994) 'The management of the induction of newly qualified teachers in primary schools.' *Journal of Education for Teaching*, **20**(3).

Turner, M.A. (1995) 'The role of mentors and teacher tutors in school-based teacher education and induction. In Kerry, T. and Mayes, A.S. (eds) (1995).

Veenman, S. (1984) 'Perceived problems of the beginning teacher.' *Review of Educational Research*, **54**(2).

Vonk, J.H.C. (1983) 'The problems of the beginning teacher.' *European Journal of Teacher Education*, **6**(2).

Watkins, C. and Whalley, C. (1993) 'Mentoring beginning teachers – issues for schools to anticipate and manage.' *School Organisation*, **13**(2).

Watkins, C. and Whalley, C. (1993) *Mentoring: Resources for School-based Development*. London: Longman.

Wilkin, M. (ed.) (1992) *Mentoring in Schools*. London: Kogan Page.

Williams, A. (1993) 'Teacher perceptions of their needs in the context of developing school-based initial teacher education.' *British Educational Research Journal*, **19**(4).

Chapter 6

Mentoring

Much has been published recently on the subject of mentoring (Wilkin, 1992; McIntyre, Hagger and Wilkin, 1993; Smith and West-Burnham, 1993; Field and Field, 1994; Yeomans and Sampson, 1994; Fish, 1995; Kerry and Mayes, 1995; Tomlinson, 1995; Edwards and Collison, 1996) and it is not my intention to replicate this. Experience shows that definitions, role descriptions and analyses of past mentoring schemes are not what most teachers taking on the role are looking for. They want to know why they are doing it, how they can best achieve the demands of the role and what is in it for them, their mentees, the school and of course their students. After a brief introduction, I set out to examine these issues for mentors at all levels in teaching, from those who are 'looking after' or supervising trainees to those senior colleagues who act as consultants to new head teachers.

Introduction

There has been an explosion of interest in the concept of mentoring in teaching and elsewhere in the past ten years (Clutterbuck, 1991; Shea, 1992; Parsloe, 1995). This has occurred across the professions and in the worlds of business and commerce. The reasons are perhaps connected with the increasing need for companies to train and develop their own staff in their own way in order both to meet rapidly changing knowledge and practices and to keep their own distinctive identities and contributions in their sector.

Apprenticeship, the preferred training mode of the New Right (Lawlor, 1990; O'Hear, 1988), has all but disappeared from the training and development scene and anyway would be considered inappropriate by professionals. Staff training and development is increasingly managed internally. Learning from somebody who knows the job and the workplace whilst actually doing the job is more appropriate. This model is to be seen in the law where new lawyers undergo pupilage, in hospitals where junior doctors undertake medical work whilst being able to observe senior colleagues, and in police work and nursing, where trained probationers are given a mentor/tutor who guides them whilst they carry out the job. The role of the mentor in teaching is clearly similar to these – guiding a trainee or newly qualified teacher through the stages of doing the job, also inducting them into the school, the district and the profession and training them in the development of professional skills.

In industry and commerce some companies (e.g. ICI, Jaguar, North West Water, British Telecom, American Express) give each new employee a mentor who keeps an eye on their progress through the company and acts as a sponsor, patron and guide to career development. The regular meetings these mentors hold with their mentees are concerned with problem-solving and suggesting routes through company procedures rather than with direct training. The advantages of this are clear – the mentor has a broad vision of the profession and a depth of experience in the company. The seniority of the mentor enables them to give the mentee access to other senior colleagues where appropriate and allows them to suggest future career moves to both the mentee and the appointing colleague. The disadvantages are that the mentee only sees the mentor occasionally and this is problematic when the biggest need most new colleagues have is for instant answers to 'silly' everyday questions with which they do not wish to embarrass themselves by asking their line managers. The nearest parallel I can find to this in the teaching profession is in the induction/mentoring of new heads of department, deputy heads and head teachers, though the role is usually performed by peers rather than senior colleagues. (There are also special mentoring schemes for women and black employees designed to break patterns of under-representation and 'the glass ceiling', which I will discuss later in this chapter.)

Mentoring trainees and newly qualified teachers

For trainee teachers or newly qualified colleagues the mentor will probably be a senior colleague who is able to commit time to: listening to the mentees' concerns and answering their questions; demonstrating and explaining; observing performance and giving feedback; discussing problems and dilemmas; giving advice and setting targets for further development.

The word 'mentor' in education has many meanings in many different applications and contexts. The Department of Education and Science first introduced the role of designated teacher to encompass some of the roles for Bolam's (1976) recommended teacher tutors of probationers – who were essentially mentors. Other early uses of the term have been: a school-based tutor jointly appointed by the university to supervise students on school-based practice and experience (Lacey, 1977); the school-based tutor appointed by the school responsible for a licensed teacher; or a person appointed by the employing authority as an outside and independent source of advice for probationary teachers (Burke and Schmidt, 1984). It is also used to describe a pro-active senior colleague engaged in actively training new teachers without an evaluative role (Heath-Camp and Camp, 1990); resource persons, problem-solvers, evaluators and providers (Godley, 1987); and examplars – successful teachers who share grade level and subject matter and who work in close proximity to the new teachers (Huling-Austin, 1986). Huffman and Leak (1986) use the word mentor to mean the identified person in each school responsible for working collaboratively with all probationers and giving them advice and support. Other titles used to describe this role include the American term 'buddy' teacher (Stone (1987) and Goodman's (1987) 'peer teacher' or 'school-based colleague').

Maw (1975) argued for a professional tutor to manage and support the induction process for new teachers and for teacher tutors to be responsible for ongoing professional development. He suggests that if the system is going to work it should be operated by a teacher who is given high status within the school (and thus probably someone who is responsible for all staff development) in order that new teachers' status within the school is not diminished. Andrews (1986) has argued that the mentor – at the most sophisticated level of the title – becomes: exemplar – demonstrating teaching and management techniques; peer supervisor – observing and giving feedback; curriculum management adviser – helping with lesson and longer-term planning; supervisor of classroom research – encouraging the reflective practitioner; and also provider of a resource and consultancy service.

Parsloe (1995) quotes extensively from a CNAA report of the late 1980s which summarizes the best uses of mentoring in its national survey of the university system but which can be applied to almost any mentoring scheme, including that used in teacher training:

> There are many views and definitions of the role of mentor, but all include verbs like support, guide, facilitate, etc. Important aspects are to do with listening, questioning and enabling, as distinct from telling, directing and restricting. Mentors are crucial to good telling, directing and restricting ... High Quality mentoring is concerned with competence, experience and clear role definition, but it also crucially depends upon the right balance of personal qualities ... good mentors are:
> 1. good motivators, perceptive, able to support the objectives of the programme and fulfil their responsibilities to the candidate;
> 2. high performers, secure in their own position within the organisation and unlikely to feel threatened by, or resentful of, the candidate's opportunities;
> 3. able to show that a responsibility for mentoring is part of their job description;
> 4. able to establish a good and professional relationship, be sympathetic, accessible and knowledgeable about the candidate's area of interest;
> 5. sufficiently senior to be in touch with the corporate structure, sharing the company's values and able to give the candidate access to resources and information;
> 6. good teachers, able to advise and instruct without interfering, allowing candidates

to explore and pursue ideas even though they may not be optimum pathways;
7. good negotiators, willing and able to plan alongside their own management teams and academics. (Parsloe, 1995, pp. 71–2)

Anderson and Shannon (in Kerry and Mayes, 1995) analyse the classical derivation of Mentor from the *Odyssey* and come up with the following strands of meaning:

> First, mentoring is an *intentional process*. Second, mentoring is a *nurturing process* which fosters the growth and development of the protégé towards full maturity ... Third, mentoring is an *insightful process* in which the wisdom of the mentor is acquired and applied by the protégé ... Fourth, mentoring is *a supportive, protective process*. (p. 28)

They go on to say mentoring can be best defined as:

> a nurturing process in which a more skilled or more experienced person, serving as a role model, teaches, sponsors, encourages, counsels and befriends a less skilled or less experienced person for the purpose of promoting the latter's professions and/or personal development. Mentoring functions are carried out within the context of an ongoing, caring relationship between the mentor and the protégé. (p. 29)

This latter seems to me to contain all the important elements of what mentoring is at present in education, so I will accept it as our working definition for this chapter.

The role of the mentor

In the United States, Hunter (1988) undertook a major literature search on the subject of the induction of new teachers and collated the following suggestions about the personal qualities of mentors and essential aspects of their roles:

1. Mentors should be congenial, helpful and have concern for the beginning teacher. (Driscoll et al., 1985)
2. Mentors should be 'considered successful by the principal'. (Huling-Austin, 1986)
3. Mentors should 'teach the same grade level and subject as the first year teacher ... and have his/her classroom located in the same area of the building.' (Huling-Austin, 1986).
4. A 'one-to-one' relationship needs to be established. (Driscoll, et al., 1985)
5. Teachers and mentors need to plan together and should be paired with like personalities. (Huling-Austin, 1986)

Wildman (1989), reporting on the role of mentors, suggested that it was to offer a range of support to new teachers. In particular they helped beginners:

1. to learn about teaching;
2. to feel good about teaching;
3. to manage their workloads;
4. to become part of the school community: and
5. they were often friends who gave personal support.

One recent paper on the role of the mentor as an important part of the induction

process has been that of Haigh (1991), reporting on his research into the management of induction in Birmingham. Haigh describes how each school in Birmingham
is asked by the LEA to appoint a mentor for probationers. In one of the schools
investigated, it was the deputy head who acted as mentor and Haigh comments that
he 'goes to each probationer for half a day each week. One week he will work with
them collaboratively and the next he will release them to observe or read documents.' The head of that school, commenting on the scheme's effectiveness,
emphasized that 'It's all timetabled. If I don't timetable it – it won't happen.' Haigh
goes on to give the viewpoint of one new teacher within the Birmingham scheme
who had negotiated an individual programme of induction with his mentor: 'I have
a mentor and we have worked out a programme of subjects to talk about such as
discipline and personal development.'

Abell (1995) found that interns needed mentors who 'support them as fledgling
teachers … assume flexible roles and adapt their roles based on interns needs'.
Cameron-Jones and O'Hara (1995) report that students who worked with mentors
who were trained and had release time to help them had a more positive attitude to
teaching and achieved higher results in their final assessments. These findings
influenced the government's decision to implement a national mentoring scheme
for trainee teachers in Scotland from September 1995. Hegarty and Simco (1995)
found that the most effective way in which mentors could help new teachers was
through 'the gift of language'. They conclude: 'This language, applied to the
unpacking of craft knowledge both enhances and validates the [practitioner]'
(p. 74). McNamara (1995), in examining who influences trainee teachers, takes a
more limited view when he suggests that the mentor's special role and area of
influence is in offering 'that particular advice about the circumstances of the class
and the children that the student should bear in mind when planning to support and
foster learning' (p. 60).

Evans et al. (1996) examined the role of mentors in HE-administered programmes of initial teacher training as compared with school-administered
programmes. Their findings are rather mixed in that they found that where
mentoring was being properly used by trained mentors, with release time to do the
work, it was very effective, but they also found that more commonly, 'schools are
failing to compensate for higher education's reduced input because they have
insufficient time and resources for mentoring of the quality which was intended by
the reforms' (p. 46).

Selecting and training mentors

Bolam (1976) proposed the idea of teacher tutors and suggested that they should
have training on appointment to the role and also have ongoing INSET support.
Training for teacher tutors was supported by Cobban (1976), who argued that the

greatest help that could be given to probationers was to have their lessons observed objectively (by a trained observer) and then to get helpful and positive feedback. Bolam (1977) went on to propose that teacher tutors should be properly trained in 'clinical supervision' (citing Cogan, 1973). Training for teacher tutors would be a 90-hour course aimed at increasing professional skills and would include: analysis of teaching, counselling adults, clinical supervision and microteaching.

The TIPS project evaluators (Bolam, Baker and McMahon, 1979) supported this, saying that in order to carry out their functions they should be trained in the major skills concerned in classroom observation – such as clinical supervision and inter-personal communication. Smyth and McCabe (1980) reported that there was much good work of this kind being achieved in Northumberland first schools by well-trained teacher tutors and later they went on to opine (in Smyth and McCabe, 1981) that induction in Northumberland was succeeding largely as a result of the commitment of experienced teacher tutors.

An apparently contrasting point of view was expressed by primary teachers in the ILEA in their research report (1980) where they were not totally convinced of the efficacy of 'teacher tutors'' work and 51 per cent indicated that they found them of little or no use. These same teachers went on to say that they found the most valuable input was from 'working alongside experienced colleagues'. (It is important to note that in the ILEA the teacher tutor was an external or visiting tutor – so in fact there is no contradiction. Probationers learned most from their peers and colleagues – in most LEAs where the process is formalized these are described as teacher tutors or designated teachers.)

One of the problems, reported in McMahon and Bolam (1981) was that of the 73 per cent of LEAs who recommended the appointment of teacher tutors (school-based colleagues) only 42 per cent provided any kind of training, and where it was provided it was 'usually fairly basic'. The one or two LEAs who did provide training for teacher tutors usually did it out of school time – only 6 per cent of LEAs provided any release time for teacher tutors to do their jobs.

McCabe and Woodward (1982) describe a course for teacher tutors in Newcastle and suggest that, although teacher tutors were making an important contribution to induction, more training could help to maximize the effectiveness of their input.

A more radical and demanding view of mentor training is proposed by Goodman (1987) in a seminal paper entitled 'Factors in becoming a proactive elementary school teacher: a preliminary study of selected novices'. Preferring the title 'peer teacher' or simply 'colleague', Goodman suggests that the responsibilities of this 'colleague' would be to assist the novice in all aspects of his/her initiation into the profession and asserts that 'Educating teachers of this caliber will require special in-service workshops as well as graduate study' (pp. 225–6). Goodman is supported in this by Huling-Austin, who conducted a major literature survey on the qualities required of mentors and concluded:

> To be able to effectively guide a novice teacher, they need to be knowledgeable about recent literature in teaching, teacher socialization/preparation, child psychology, curriculum theory/design, and learning theories. At the same time they should have training in facilitative learning, creative problem solving and other 'human relations' abilities. (Huling-Austin, 1986).

The need for mentors and mentees to share the same general conditions was confirmed by Huffman and Leak (1986) (who use the term mentor to mean 'a teacher colleague selected to support a new teacher'). They found in their research that the most effective mentors were those who taught the same subject content to the same grade and were given conference time with their new teacher charges.

Blair and Bercik (1987) declared that in order to achieve success mentors needed more than their present superficial level of training. They suggest that mentors needed training in demonstrating teaching, observing teaching and coaching teachers and they should also study teacher development, new teacher needs, effective teaching, supervision skills and professional development.

Godley (1987) looked at how mentors perceived their roles and found that they saw themselves as most successful in being resource persons, problem-solvers, evaluators and providers. In his observation, however, Godley found that mentors appeared to be most successful when sharing interpersonal skills, nurturing a collegial relationship with beginning teachers and when sharing process skills. This has implications for training and for increasing self-examination and reflectiveness amongst mentors.

Heath-Camp and Camp (1990) suggested assigning a mentor, who was preferably a veteran teacher in the same field, to each new teacher. Once this relationship was established, mutual observation was recommended, and a pro-active role for the mentor in regularly seeking out and offering help and advice to the new teacher.

Rowie Shaw's *Teacher Training in Secondary Schools* (1992) usefully includes a job description for a mentor and goes on to include selection criteria. They should:

1. be a teacher with recent and relevant experience of at least one year;
2. be able to demonstrate up-to-date knowledge and expertise in the content of their subject;
3. be able to demonstrate knowledge and use of a variety of teaching methods and enable others to use them;
4. be able to demonstrate an active interest in pursuing their own professional development;
5. be able to work collaboratively in various teams as a voluntary partner;
6. be able to communicate effectively with a variety of individuals and groups;
7. be committed to the promotion of equal opportunities through teaching and training;
8. have interpersonal skills which enable others to relate to them as a guide, counsellor and assessor;
9. be able to identify and help others to identify good practice in classroom teaching (their own and that of others);

10. have a knowledge of evaluation and assessment techniques including self-assessment for teachers and pupils;
11. be able to organise their own time and that of others. (pp. 136–7)

Smith and West-Burnham (1993) offer a list of the skills mentors would need and suggestions for training programmes to meet those needs (pp. 22 and 38). Combined, they make a useful checklist for mentor trainers:

Observing
Listening
Providing positive feedback
Negotiating
Problem-solving
Managing stress
Target-setting
Advice-giving
Linking theory and practice
Organizing and managing learning programmes
Maintaining a productive professional relationship

Yeomans and Sampson (1994), analysing the results of their survey of the role of mentors in training licensed and articled teachers, make the following observations:

> Mentors need to be effective teachers because a key dimension of their role is to provide student teachers with a model of effective teaching, including key skills such as curriculum planning, classroom control, organisation and pedagogy . . . [They need] enabling, interpersonal and analytic as well as pedagogic skills . . . Mentors need status and credibility in the school . . . In short, when choosing mentors, head teachers will need to consider carefully how far existing responsibilities allow potential mentors to perform multiple roles effectively, recognizing that being a mentor can be relevant experience for staff hoping to move into primary school management. (pp. 204–5)

In the same year Les Tickle (1994) listed 'Essential qualities for teacher tutors' (surprisingly he doesn't use the word 'mentor' in his book) as:

Professional standing
Credibility as a teacher
Experience

Pastoral
Empathy
Sympathy
Sensitivity

Personal/Relational
Approachability
Sense of humour
Good listener
Calm manner

Tutorial
Accessibility/availability
Positive constructive nature
Supportive/encouraging
Honesty
Reliability

Clearly mentors need to be skilful and experienced professionals committed to the idea of continuing professional development for their mentees and themselves. They need to be able to listen, to model planning, teaching and reflection as well as being able to help mentees learn by emulation, self-direction and reflection on action. Those who set out to plan programmes for mentors should be aware of and sensitive to the wide variety of educational and practical experience the mentors bring with them. Differentiation at this level is difficult but analysis of needs and provision of choice and range can help all to learn what they need and not feel their experience is being ignored.

It becomes clear to those of us who train mentors that many of them could benefit from having mentors themselves because they lead difficult and stressful lives; they have professional development needs and they would like to have someone to talk to about their work. I refer to this topic in Chapter 7 whilst examining continuing professional development.

What do mentors get out of mentoring?

Andrews (1987) proposed five ways in which mentors would benefit from undertaking their role as providers of probationer induction within schools. These can be summarized as:

1. Modelling different instructional methodologies [gaining constructive feedback on own teaching];
2. Providing regular observation and feedback [thus experiencing peer supervision];
3. Working jointly on the introduction of new curriculum materials [thus gaining from new teachers' recent studies and gaining curriculum management expertise];
4. Engaging in classroom research [taking part in and encouraging critical reflection in teaching];
5. Acting as a resource and consultant [gaining experience in educational consultancy]. (pp. 150–1)

The mentor's view of the process is also examined by Crawley (1990) in an interesting overview which encompasses her own induction and her role as teacher tutor. She says of her role and training as teacher tutor:

> The consultancy aspect of the teacher tutor role was enjoyable, talking things through with the probationer and planning and organising their release times ... We formed good relationships and I found the role sometimes required me to act as go-between

between the Head and probationers ... My own position in the school as an experienced member of staff who the head respected, but nonetheless a class teacher alongside the newcomers was ideal for a teacher tutor ... It was a stimulating experience both to observe another practitioner at work, to learn from them and to call on one's own professional experience and expertise to extract points for discussion ... The teacher tutor training at the beginning of the year was valuable in refining my role. Subsequent sessions on time management, observation procedures and other such issues were of personal benefit. (pp. 125–6)

Wildman (1989), reporting on the Chesterfield Beginning Mentor Programme (USA) (where mentors were selected by principals for their potential as excellent role models and because they revealed a reflective attitude to teaching), wrote of the advantages mentors felt they received from their role. He listed these as:

1. opportunities to work and talk with other teachers during mentor training;
2. participation in beginning teachers' success and progress; and
3. having the opportunity to reflect on their own teaching.

The benefits of mentoring in the professions are discussed in Smith and West-Burnham (1993) where they compare the benefits in nursing to those in teaching. For the teaching profession their list is as follows:

Mentee The benefits of mentoring include:
*   Having a medium through which to address ideas to senior management
*   Providing support, consolation, sympathy, constructive feedback
*   The opportunity to share achievements and failures
*   Time to observe other teachers at work
*   Opportunity to be reflective on performance
*   Non-threatening guidance
*   Feeling less isolated within an established staff
*   Meeting [others in the same learning situation]
*   Having someone to talk to.

Mentor The benefits of mentoring include:
*   Makes you evaluate the quality of your own teaching/planning
*   Develops appraisal skills
*   Keeping in touch with the problems of [others in the same learning situation]
*   An opportunity to be reflective on your own performance
*   Good experience for career development
*   Increased status and responsibilities
*   Increasing your enthusiasm
*   Providing new ideas

Teaching Profession The benefits of mentoring include:
*   Well adjusted teachers
*   Good networks
*   Improved relationships between staff/team building
*   Identification of communication/organization problems in the school
*   Likely to entice more people into profession and improve its status (Smith and West-Burnham, 1993, p. 19. Our changes in parentheses.)

Another little-recognized but nevertheless significant effect of mentoring is the evidence that it may reduce the numbers leaving the profession in the first few years (Littleton and Littleton, 1988; Quaglia, 1989; Odell and Ferraro, 1992) and thus provide stability, making staff development a viable investment and school improvement more likely.

Mentoring is an important staff development activity, claim Keely, Beck and apThomas (in Kerry and Mayes, 1995) because:

> To be a mentor is to contribute to one's own self development.
> Helping others to reflect must be beneficial to oneself.
> After questioning your own practice there must be the challenge of doing something about it.
> Developing . . . skills (e.g. listening, giving feedback, observing practice, coaching, counselling, motivating, diagnosing performance, etc.) can only help enhance performance in other areas of your work.
> Delivery of INSET on site is valuable staff development for those involved.
> Mentor status can enhance [mentors'] self-esteem, self-confidence and self-image.
> Role modelling and helping others develop by example ensures you think carefully about your own practice. (pp. 257–8)

It is the process of deliberate thought about one's work both to prepare it for others to observe, comment on and question and the post-event discussion of its relative success and ways to improve or progress the achieved results which has become the focus for much discussion in recent years. The key concept is that it is through reflection on action that improvement in practice is achieved and one of the key ways to learn to reflect is through having reflective practice modelled for one by a mentor.

The reflective mentor and the reflective teacher

Although the idea of the 'reflective teacher' had been widely discussed in the literature before (e.g. Schön, 1983; Pollard and Tann, 1987), the first discussion of any significance of the concept as it applied to beginning teachers and their mentors came up in a paper by Goodman (1987). She proposed that, however good their initial training as pro-active and reflective practitioners, beginning teachers 'may not be able to act upon many of their decisions until they have gained more experience' (p. 212). She went on to propose a role for improved induction and mentoring: 'Perhaps most novice teachers could become reflective decision makers given the right type of pre-service education and school based induction programme' (p. 226).

This theme of the role of the mentor in developing reflective teachers is picked up by Tickle (1988), where he expounds on the need for reflective mentors to be part of a research-based induction programme in order to increase the professionalism of teachers. It could be achieved, Tickle proposes, by 'improvement of practice based on investigating and understanding that practice' (p. 97). The importance of choosing reflective teachers as mentors is emphasized again by Tickle (1989), who asserts that it is the only way to ensure that new teachers themselves become reflective. There is a need for deliberate socialization – where new teachers were left to socialize themselves within the profession through trial and error there was a tendency for them to develop idiosyncratic coping strategies which led to anxiety, frustration and even failure (see Lacey, 1977). Tickle (1989) proposes a clear role for the reflective mentor when he claims that new teacher success is linked with 'capacity for reflection-in-action [being] recognised and developed with support from colleagues who are themselves reflective practitioners' (p. 284). In the United States, Quaglia (1989) came to similar conclusions in reviewing the differences between new teacher expectations of teaching and their actual experience. In his conclusions he proposed: 'Knowledge of the foundations of education, child and adolescent growth and development, pedagogy, theory and research need to be joined with the realities of the classroom to prepare "reflective practitioners"' (p. 6).

A good summary of the contemporary views on mentoring for reflective teaching in teacher training and assessment is offered by Fish (1995), who rejects the British government's Technical Rational (TR) view of development based on the achievement of what she sees as behaviouristic competences in favour of the reflective practitioner view, 'a complex, dynamic social activity with a moral dimension ... '. Fish proposes that helping the student to learn practice involves the mentor in:

- acknowledging and trying to understand this complexity
- seeking to articulate, and keep under review, a clear principled base to personal practice (and recognising that practice itself can often fall short of this)
- knowing how research on teaching and learning can enlighten practice
- knowing how to investigate practice, how to unearth theory from it and how to reflect upon it, theorise about it and challenge it with formal theory
- understanding how individual practice relates to the moral and traditional aspects of professional practice and recognising the implications of this for teaching
- being able to draw out of the student the idea, beliefs, assumptions and values that lie at the base of that student's practice
- being able to help the student to find new approaches to practice and their rationales
- being able to help the student find his/her own preferred approach to professional practice
- being able to engage in discussions with the student about the purposes of education, in order to enable the student to explore how his/her own practice relates to the moral and social tradition of teaching. (pp. x–xi)

I would like to conclude this section on mentoring as a way of developing the reflective practitioner by endorsing Fish's view that 'the mentor can help the student towards becoming a member of the teaching profession rather than simply becoming a proficient performer in an individual classroom'. Before looking at the way in which mentoring can be used in continuing professional development I examine some of the problems in the process of mentoring.

Tensions and dilemmas in mentoring

One of the perennial tensions within the mentor/professional tutor/buddy role complex is the concern with how assessment is built into the system and who should carry it out – there is little doubt that it always affects the relationship but equally the person who assesses the new teacher needs to know their work well enough to make an informed judgement. Perhaps it is for this reason that some researchers argue that the mentor and not the head teacher or principal is best placed to assess probationers.

Bolam et al. (1979) suggest a compromise in the assessment dilemma – that teacher tutors should not be responsible for assessment but that they should be consulted before reports are written. Heath-Camp and Camp (1990) are quite clear in their opinions on the dilemma of using the mentor as the new teacher's evaluator and warn that it should never be done.

Another ongoing dilemma for teacher tutors – the tension between encouraging individual development and inducing compliance to the norms of the school – is pointed out in Dorner (1979), where she critically assesses her own induction year. Lacey had examined this dilemma in some detail in his *The Socialization of Teachers* (1977) when he developed his concept of social strategies, 'strategic compliance, internalised adjustment and strategic re-definition' which trainees (and by implication new teachers) adopted to survive. Davis (1980) picks this up, together with Bolam's earlier concern with the teacher tutor's divided loyalties, to provide pastoral support for the new teacher whilst avoiding any assessment role. Davis argued that the probationers in his sample felt that the teacher tutor should provide direct training, based on observed needs, in order to help them remedy weaknesses and develop competencies.

Spooner (1984) revisits the issue of the balance staff tutors need to maintain between pastoral and training roles (or between 'encouraging and intervening' as he puts it) and exposes the paradox that it is the better teachers who make the most of advice, whilst the poorer 'wrap themselves in the mantle of professional pride to cover their threadbare talents'.

In a discussion of professional development across a range of professions, Eraut (1985) identifies one of the key dilemmas for new teachers as the need for professional autonomy in tension with feelings of isolation – often occurring at a time when the new teacher's first school appointment demands a change in teaching style. This issue is further discussed in Kramer-Hayon (1987) where she looks at the unusually isolated position of teachers vis-à-vis other new professionals (citing doctors and engineers who, she asserts, tend to work more in co-operative situations). The new teacher, Kramer-Hayon claims, is torn between the need to demonstrate professional independence and the awareness of their, initially frequent, dependence on colleagues for advice and information.

Training teacher tutors (mentors) to provide improved induction for new teachers is another dilemma discussed by Wubbels, Creton and Hooymayer (1987), who suggest that this training should be carried out by teacher training institutions. In their research they found that although levels of anxiety and stress in new teachers were not reduced by having a teacher tutor (indeed in some cases they were slightly higher), new teachers who were guided by college-trained teacher tutors expressed a greater level of satisfaction with their induction. Wubbels et al. go on to propose that teacher trainers should also be employed as part of the induction process, because 'experienced teachers who are induction mentors generally do not have sufficient time, skills or know how to give adequate and satisfactory guidance to young teachers who are facing severe disciplinary problems' (p. 93).

As I come to the conclusion of the chapter on mentoring in which I have discussed its growth from an aspect of initial teacher training, I will discuss the role of mentoring in staff continuing development and as a tool for whole-school improvement. Kelly, Beck and ap Thomas (in Wilkin, 1992) refer to this process as mentoring in the 'Learning School' making a comparison with the ideas of Pedlar et al. (1989), who describe 'The Learning Company' as one which 'facilitates the learning of all its members and continuously transforms itself'. They go on to list the qualities which Learning Companies display.

> Such organizations:
> a) have a climate in which individual members are encouraged to learn and to develop their full potential;
> b) extend this learning to include customers (pupils?), suppliers (parents?) and other significant stakeholders (Governors and community?) wherever possible:
> c) make human resource development strategy central to business policy;
> d) have a continuous process of organizational transformation harnessing the fruits of individual learning. (Wilkin, 1992, p. 178)

There has been a clear movement towards this, with many schools beginning to see themselves as 'learning organizations', with staff development and school improvement high on their agendas. Whether parental choice, the publication of examination and SATs results, government pressure or the demands of OFSTED have led to this is debatable. But staff development as a means to school improvement is happening and many schools are moving towards gaining the attainment of the Investing in People kitemark.

Most recently there has been a decline in the role of higher education in the training and development of teacher mentors since the demise of funding from the Teacher Training Agency which provided funds for their training under transitional funding intended to aid the transfer of teacher training to a more school-based approach. Whether this will lead to a complete phasing out of HE influence on mentors remains to be seen, but there is evidence that schools are reluctant to spend their increasingly scarce INSET and GEST funding on day-release courses in HE establishments. Perhaps the future is in the kind of project we have begun with a group of school professional development tutors in which we are using university research funding to plan induction programmes, professional development schemes and research jointly. The proposed outcome of this will be joint publications which investigate the practical outcomes from our discussions of theoretical principles.

The role of mentors in continuing professional development

The argument for the induction mentor becoming professional development tutor was endorsed by Wilson and D'Arcy (1987) who felt that it was the best way to raise the low level of perceived importance of teacher tutors within schools and within induction programmes.

Rowie Shaw (1992) was amongst the first to pull all the threads together and to see how the expense of training mentors for licensed teachers, student teachers and inductees was one which could best be recouped by using those trained people as 'super mentors' for 'generic mentoring'. She puts her case for using these mentors for school improvement thus:

> The skills required for mentoring are highly specialised and in some cases have been on a par with the skills which teacher trainers develop over many years' experience. It would be difficult to deploy a system whereby a large group of teachers was trained to be mentors on expensive courses run by H.E. every year. Yet ... there is a core of these skills which, if deployed consistently in our schools, could assist in training and development throughout every stage in a teacher's career, including the support and supervision of staff and pupils as well as appraisal and to which every manager should have access. This is the concept of generic mentoring. (p. 72)

Shaw claims that the benefits to schools of using generic mentoring would include:

- raising awareness about classroom practice;
- providing a climate for a discussion about teaching methods and subject content;
- the enhancement of a variety of school processes, all of which lead to an improved classroom experience for pupils with an ensuing rise in achievement. (p. 76)

She also claims that schools can expect better retention of staff by offering improved rewards and opportunities and better job satisfaction. Benefiting staff, she asserts, benefits schools, which leads to improved pupil performance. This is surely a message which schools, presently under the scrutiny of parents, press, government and OFSTED, will want to consider.

We have had considerable experience of mentors who have found that the role has given them new impetus in their own teaching, new interest in continuing their own professional development and a new status in their schools. Recently I have supervised MA students who have, starting from the role of mentor, become professional development tutors with an interest in school improvement through the use of mentoring in continuing professional development. These mentors have written induction programmes, planned continuing professional development pro-grammes for the school embracing appraisal and school development, and worked with universities to secure recognition and accreditation for the work their col-leagues have undertaken. In one case a school has undertaken a modular in-service scheme leading to a school-centred MA course (with tutorial support and valida-tion from a university but effectively taught and run in-house). The mentor/staff development officer for this scheme gained an early promotion to a deputy headship in a school looking for school improvement through staff development.

In other schools Anglia Polytechnic University has supported there has been a commitment to the idea of profiling as a means of ensuring continuing professional development, with mentoring playing a key role in ensuring that the process works. One newly qualified teacher has moved within five years through mentoring to professional tutor in charge of school improvement using peer mentoring/appraisal as the means of encouraging the reflection necessary to underpin planned continu-ing professional development. The profiles of reflection and achievement which individuals keep are then the basis of review with her and the head teacher as a means of keeping the momentum of school improvement.

It seems to me that mentoring, as a professionally owned and monitored means of ensuring continuing professional development, is one of the growth areas in training and development (and one of the key routes to gaining promotion in today's schools). Any professionals who can offer non-threatening and effective means to school improvement and who have the skills to help colleagues develop their own expertise through reflection and profiling achievement will find them-selves in demand. In an era when school inspection, assessment and appraisal have gained reputations of externally imposed compliance to government and manage-ment dictats, mentoring would appear to be a beacon of professionalism to embattled teachers.

Another area where mentoring has made a significant contribution to school improvement has been the support of newly appointed head teachers by colleagues who act as mentors during their first year. This has been shown to be more effective than many head teacher training programmes because advice given is specific and context-related.

I am at present involved in evaluating a mentoring scheme as part of the Opportunities 2000 initiative aimed at getting more women into the senior eche-lons of higher education. Mentors have been selected to support the development of women who wish to become senior managers and a programme of meetings has been set up in order that discussion, modelling, networking and advice can be given to support these women in their attempts to 'get through the glass ceiling'. Although the scheme is only at an early stage there are clear signs that it is being accepted as helpful training for the women mentees and is also offering benefits for the mentors. The following section is an executive summary of the preliminary interim research findings.

Anglia Polytechnic University's 'Women into Management' mentoring scheme

Under the auspices of Dr Jill Dimmock and the Equal Opportunities Committee the Anglia mentoring scheme was set up in June 1996 to encourage women in the university to become more involved in management at a senior level.

Mike Malone-Lee, Anglia Polytechnic University's new vice chancellor, not only approves of the women's mentoring scheme but is playing an active part in it, acting as a mentor. His views on mentoring are both well informed and liberal.

> It is one of my personal targets to increase the number of women in senior management at this university. I've acted as a mentor before, in my previous job in the Civil Service, but not specifically in a women's mentoring scheme. As a mentor you have to have experience to share, you have to be able to listen and to allow yourself to be led in the relationship to where the mentee wants to go. One has to be open-minded and not attempt to impose solutions or suggest you know the truth.

Dr Mike Turner undertook to monitor the progress of the scheme and this report briefly describes his initial findings on the early stages of the mentoring scheme. Eight pairs of mentors and mentees were interviewed and their views analysed for key issues and dilemmas.

The first reaction of all interviewed is that they are pleased, impressed and even excited by the scheme.

> As far as we're concerned it's going well. The scheme itself is a great adventure. (Mentor A)

> I'm enjoying it and getting on well with [my mentor]. I knew her before. (Mentee Z)

What's been happening?

The scheme has begun very well with everybody gaining something and all pairs having met and begun the process. The original intention of weekly meetings has not been achieved and most pairs are managing monthly meetings. Several interviewees felt that shorter more frequent meetings would be better if that could be achieved.

Most have spent the early sessions getting to know one another though there have also been programmes set up, tours of other sites, work shadowing and direct input.

How did mentors see their role?

Most mentor interviewees spoke of their role as enablers – helping other people to develop:

> APU needs more women in senior posts ... having a mentoring scheme should help. (Mentor G)

> One mentor felt that the mentoring scheme would help the university:
> It should help organizational learning. We don't foster or encourage a corporate approach and mentoring is one way we can help that a little. (Mentor H)

What do mentees expect from the scheme?

Most focused on building relationships and networking, gaining knowledge and building confidence rather than direct expectations of promotion. Comments included:

> My aims include: take advantage of another's experience and get insight into working at Anglia at a senior level ... [and] build my self confidence. (Mentee T)

> The development of a friendship outside my department – gaining a broader perspective ... and a richer insight, e.g. into people my mentor knows, from different angles. (Mentee X)

What's in it for mentors?

Mentors were committed to equal opportunities and management development for women. They wanted to support a university initiative. Other outcomes perceived included gaining a professional friend, satisfaction in helping others and an awareness of benefits for themselves:

> The added bonus is reflection on our own work. When people ask you to justify your actions you do begin to reconsider. (Mentor G)

> [I enjoy] seeing people grow. I nurture people who have potential ... I'm keen to help women develop in the university. Also I get more experience in being a mentor and expand my repertoire. (Mentor D)

How well were participants prepared for the scheme by the university?

Almost everyone felt that the university training and paperwork had been good and all appreciated how well it had been prepared and delivered. Some were unable to attend the training or briefing sessions. Access to training courses was seen as 'an important issue for a multi-site university'. Some were satisfied with the training but felt it was too long before the scheme actually started:

Preparation suffered a little because of the summer break – we received preliminary papers in the summer term ... but the long break led to a hiatus before the formal launch in October – thus a loss of initial impetus. (Mentee S)

Some wished for further support and training:

It has been very difficult for my mentor and I to plan ahead for what to focus on. Perhaps some structure or a list of ideas [would be helpful]. (Mentor T)

Suggested changes and improvements

1. Improve the launch and partner introduction.
2. Provide more information and more ideas for mentoring activities.
3. Improve the timing schedule of the scheme. Several interviewees commented on the gap between introduction and actual mentoring.
4. Formal group meetings of mentors and of mentees should happen in work time (especially given the problems of working mothers) and these meetings should be timetabled. There should be at least one mentor/mentee meeting a month.
5. Selection of mentees should involve more positive selection and not rely on volunteers. Some mentees should be chosen and actively encouraged by managers.

Conclusions and key issues

There was a consensus amongst interviewees that this was an important and necessary scheme and that it should continue next year. Some felt that one year wasn't enough and wanted to keep their mentors. Everyone praised the idea of giving women opportunities to become managers though some wondered if volunteers were necessarily the right people to be mentored – given that lack of confidence was one of the things holding many women back. Others felt that the university mentoring scheme for new staff should be properly revived and structured so that it happened more consistently. Many felt that everyone needed a mentor and that the structure of relationships and inter-departmental networking in the university would be improved and greater corporate identity achieved if mentoring was more widely employed. All looked forward to seeing more women in the senior management structure of the university as a result of this initiative.

Chapter 7

Continuing Professional Development

Initial teacher education (ITE) and in-service education for teachers (INSET) are increasingly viewed as two aspects of a single process which can be labelled as continuous professional development. The newly qualified teacher is merely at the first stage of a developmental process which may travel different paths depending upon the particular needs of both the teacher and the school. Yet, this is not the conventional image held: the qualified practitioner, whether teacher, doctor or lawyer, is judged to be competent at the job from day one – and is, supposedly, assessed as such at the culmination of a programme of initial training. In England and Wales, doctors are registered with the General Medical Council, solicitors become full members of the Law Society, and a teacher receives official recognition through being assigned a number by the Department for Education and Employment. Qualified status is therefore granted on the basis of a summative judgement as to 'competency' and is not generally dependent on periodic reassessment linked to compulsory up-dating of knowledge, retraining, etc. In certain cases, qualified status and the licence to practise can be revoked, usually for reasons of professional misconduct and relevant criminal acts.

If nothing else, this is a curious conception of the learning process and of the nature of knowledge. According to this view, learning in any broad, structured sense ceases with the attainment of the initial qualification since what is needed to be known constitutes a prescribed package which is subject to change as a result of new knowledge being accepted as conventional wisdom only after many years. Ironically, critics of initial teacher education have frequently attacked it for being all too ready to take on board fashions in theory, whether neo-Marxist views on educational achievement or the 'real books' approach to the teaching of reading.

Learning from experience?

This, of course, is at variance with the experience of many teachers who accept that they will continue to learn about the business throughout their working life. But this picture of continuous professional development in England and Wales has been one of learning on the job in a particularistic manner, a significant number of teachers attending short courses, conferences, etc. provided by LEAs and other bodies, and a few studying on long, award-bearing programmes. This has resulted in a variably qualified teaching force which has not necessarily been a reflection either of competences gained or of relevant learning experiences. To the extent that many teachers will have undergone learning experiences either as a result of attendance at short courses, in-service days, or through the course of their work responsibilities at school it was recognized that much of INSET provision in reality lay outside the province of the traditional providers of higher education. The situation was in fact not too dissimilar to that which has conventionally characterized vocational and professional education as a whole in the UK. This can be summarized as one where organizations have often jealously guarded their own practices, and training was to be concerned therefore with induction into the specifics of those practices rather than into broader, and sometimes more theoretical, perspectives. The sometimes understandable fear of good workers being poached by competitor organizations could be mitigated by ensuring that such workers were trained solely in the working practices of the particular firm.

Given this and the developing competition between higher education institutions, the accreditation of prior learning (APL) and the accreditation of prior *experiential* learning (APEL) soon became important elements of a new approach to INSET. The growth of APL recognized the importance of a number of factors affecting the professional development of teachers. First, given that study for advanced qualifications is mostly undertaken on a part-time basis, this process can often be interrupted as a result of work and domestic considerations and thus a means is needed of taking prior study into account should a teacher wish to resume at a much later date. Second, if a staged award is gained at a particular level (such as a postgraduate diploma), a teacher may wish to use it to count towards a full award (such as a master's degree). Third, APL has been viewed as an essential aid in the enhancement of geographical mobility, in enabling teachers to transfer credit gained from one institution to another.

APEL went a stage further, in its recognition of the considerable amount of learning that experienced teachers will have gained during the course of their work. For example, a teacher may have had a significant role in an aspect of curriculum development in a school, during which time a substantial amount of research and background reading needed to be undertaken and evidenced in the production of documents. Under an APEL system, a teacher training institution would be in a position to accredit such learning on the basis of a portfolio of work presented by the candidate, and thus enable a teacher to gain an advanced qualification in a much shorter time. Against this, it might be argued that higher education institutions have entered rather murky waters in taking essentially unstructured experience into consideration for the award of a qualification of national, if not international standing. The notion of academic standards is invoked to question the value of 'experiential learning', that it suggests that learning can take place outside the institutional structure of a higher education establishment. For this is learning without teaching or a process of formal assessment; it is a situation where the learner is in control of the learning process, rather than the teacher. Yet, for APEL to be an acceptable means by which teachers can make progress in gaining an advanced qualification it is recognized that quality assurance procedures need to be in place and that the universities will continue to have an important role to play.

Towards partnership in INSET

A further development has signalled a shift away from higher education institutions as the sole location for delivery, and as the sole provider of award-bearing INSET programmes. Once more, the market is invoked as a major determinant in the allocation of resources in the area of education: since it is increasingly clear that collectively planned provision and funding for higher education will cease to be the means by which postgraduate and professional courses are generated, the stimulus will move to the purchasers. In other words, the emphasis is to be on the demand side rather than the supply side where individual schools have more and more buying power, with the largest of them in a position to demand programmes, perhaps leading to an advanced qualification, to suit their particular sets of needs.

As an illustration of partnership in in-service, continuous professional development, we may cite the case of a master's degree programme designed in consultation with an English secondary school located in the South-East of England and delivered on-site to its teachers. Negotiations between representatives from the school and a locally based university to explore such a possibility began in January 1991 and culminated with the award of master's degrees in education in January 1995. The programme was experimental and, not surprisingly, a number of difficulties were experienced en route, not least concerning expectations and assumptions on the part of both teachers from the school and tutors from different departments in the university.

Initially, the university's education department was approached by the head teacher of the school who was able to spend a considerable amount of the school's budget on in-service training. He was particularly interested in the possibility of a number of his teachers being able to obtain a master's degree qualification from the university, which would be geared to the general perceived needs of the school and which could also be delivered in the 'twilight' hours (i.e. mid-afternoon, directly following the end of the school day) on the school premises. While teacher training institutions have long been used to respond to demand as far as short, non-award-bearing courses are concerned, this was a radical request since it implicitly suggested that the existing offerings from the university (including a well-established master's degree) did not meet the needs of this particular group of teachers. It challenged the assumption that *only* the university could define the content of a degree programme and that the programme had to be delivered at a time and place which did not compromise the university's control of such matters, that is, on university premises at a conventional hour which, in the case of a part-time INSET course, would be early evening. In addition, the content demanded by the school meant that another department in the university needed to be approached to discuss additional contributions to the programme.

At the time of the beginning of discussions the university had just implemented a framework for the construction of individually negotiated degree programmes where such programmes did not already exist in its portfolio. The 'Open Course Scheme' was a radical concept which raised questions of course coherence, quality assurance, and programme management, but it did provide a possible vehicle for this school-centred master's degree. The idea was that a prospective student or group of students could arrange an individually tailored programme with the university, composed of existing modules from other courses plus the occasional specially constructed module. It was clearly a venture into demand-led higher education and appeared suited to the needs of the school. By the autumn of 1991 an MA programme had been constructed, drawing upon modules from the existing M.Ed. (Educational Research) degree and, to a lesser extent, from the MSc (Educational Management) degree. The course was managed by a university tutor from the education department, who also taught some of the modules. Although a small number of the teachers originally on the programme dropped out along the way, the majority stayed the course to gain their degrees.

There were a number of indirect outcomes from this particular form of co-operation between school and university. First, it helped to solidify the relationship between the two institutions at an interpersonal level; second, it helped to pave the way for future co-operation between the school and the university in other fields (for example, in establishing a consortium for school-based postgraduate initial training); third, it contributed to the general development of university INSET provision in a demand-led direction. It is this last aspect which became significant for this university, when it was decided that if further professional development was to be meaningful for teachers it had to meet two major criteria. First, it should be closely related to institutional as well as personal needs, with an emphasis upon coping with change; second, there should be a way in which teachers could gain, through an accretion of modules, an advanced qualification. In this way, teachers need not commit themselves from the beginning to the completion of a long, award-bearing course, but rather complete individual modules at their own pace, where they provide the coherence to their pattern of learning instead of having coherence imposed from above.

Extending the frontiers

In a wider context, the development of INSET on an 'outreach' basis has indicated a move towards meeting the needs of teachers as a result of increased dialogue. Following groundwork laid by the Open University in its INSET work, distance learning in continuous professional development is also now an increasing aspect of such provision. Distance learning in the 1990s involves the use of advanced telecommunications and information technology (e.g. the Internet) in addition to the more conventional modes (printed learning packages and use of the broadcast media). A consequence of this is the possibility of a greater convergence between work, home and study.

It is fairly clear, however, that much of the impetus for extending beyond conventional INSET provision is not just the consequence of a changed and changing power relationship between schools and higher education institutions but also the direct impact of squeeze on funding. Some UK higher education institutions are now looking to satisfy a growing demand for advanced qualifications in education in countries which as yet do not appear to be in a position to meet it. Accordingly, one university has recently pioneered an accelerated INSET programme for a cohort of foreign nationals leading to bachelors' and masters' degree awards based on the provision of a residential summer school.

Teachers as learners – a cross-national view

Education has had to face the impact of global economic change, political upheaval and cultural transformation. The latter is reflected partly in disenchantment with the modernizing tendencies of the post-war era, where schools and universities – and the teachers who work in them – were considered as part of grand modernist plans for national development and prosperity. Such tendencies were not only apparent in the communist and social democratic governments of the 1950s and 1960s but also in the policies of 'one-nation' conservative governments and international agencies. Teachers in schools and universities could be viewed as experts who, indirectly at least, were able to contribute to social and economic development. The United States, sometimes seen as neo-colonialist in its approach, has, since 1945, displayed these characteristics in a marked manner, with the federal government often taking a leading role during the late 1950s and 1960s, despite objections to the fact of its interference in what was constitutionally seen as an individual state matter.

Yet, teachers continue to remain in an ambiguous social position. The continuing expertise of surgeons, for example, appears to be based upon an accumulation of technical knowledge and know-how through entry into the secret garden of the medical curriculum. Controversy over the efficacy of surgical techniques only occasionally emerges into the public domain. However, teachers' expertise, while generally considered as having a singular impact upon the capacity of children to learn in an effective manner, is constantly subjected to 'public' scrutiny.

Conclusion

In the case of continuing professional development, 'partnership' has possibly developed along somewhat different lines when compared with initial teacher education. A number of factors have converged, some of which pre-date the hegemony of the market ideology of the last twenty years or so. First of all, schools and other educational institutions have often been aware of the dissonant relationship which existed between the kinds of courses offered by universities – and even by local education authorities – and the articulated professional needs of teachers. Some teachers, no doubt, wished (and may continue to wish) to pursue postgraduate studies which would not be viewed as directly utilitarian; rather they would be primarily for personal fulfillment. On the whole, though, such studies which, twenty or more years ago, would have been funded by English local education authorities (with secondments on a full-time basis for a fortunate few) are no longer deemed appropriate in a situation where schools are the in-service budget holders. The largely academic master's degree courses – as in sociological, philosophical and historical studies of education – have been subjected to a process of de-legitimation, while modular programmes focused upon such issues as the implementation of the National Curriculum, classroom discipline and resource management, reflect institutional demand. Further professional development for teachers in England and Wales thus looks likely to continue in a number of directions which will be driven largely by the 'market', the priorities of the Teacher Training Agency and of individual schools. To what extent this will also satisfy the very real needs of teachers in respect of their broader professional identities remains to be seen.

Chapter 8

Profiling and Continuing Professional Development in Teacher Training

The intention of this chapter is to examine the way in which profiling and the concept of continuing professional development have come about and to make some suggestions about how profiles can be constructed and how they might help schools with staff development and school improvement.

Recent interest in continuing professional development in England and Wales is a timely revival of earlier concerns. Lord James (DES, 1972a) recommended a three-phase cycle of continuous professional development, and Bolam's TIPS (Teacher Induction Pilot Scheme) research (1973 and 1975a) clearly indicated the need for links between initial training and induction.

There has been much discussion recently of the need for teachers' development to be continuous from initial training throughout their careers. Andrews (1986 and 1987) referred to the need for a 'confluence' of the three phases of teacher education – initial, induction and in-service. Other recent research has highlighted growing concern for the need for properly planned and consistently carried out induction as a necessary continuing aspect of teacher education (Earley, 1992 and 1994; Turner 1992, 1993a, 1993b and 1994). The Department for Education and Employment (DfEE) and Teacher Training Agency (TTA) are beginning to move towards a National Vocational Qualification (NVQ) system of professional development. This approach uses workplace-based assessment to profile achievement of professional competence based on 'on-the-job' self-assessment monitored by a senior colleague acting as moderator/assessor instead of relying on assessment based on examinations.

The need to continue the acquisition of teacher skills and competences beyond initial training into the induction year and in-service for teachers has been the subject of recent government publications (Alexander et al., 1992; DES, 1992a and 1992b, OFSTED, 1993a). The Department for Education Administrative Memorandum 9/92 lists these competences for secondary teachers, and DES circular AM

14/93 does the same for the primary teacher. These publications have recognized that few teachers can acquire all the competences they require during their initial training and therefore need ongoing professional development in the induction year and beyond.

It is in recognition of the impossibility of providing a training (especially in the one-year PGCE courses) which totally equips a new teacher for all that they will meet in post that the Teacher Training Agency has produced a career entry profile for teachers completing initial training. These profiles, based on the teacher competences detailed in AM 9/92 (secondary) and AM 14/93 (primary), accompany NQTs to their first placement. Their main purpose is to inform employers of the new teacher's strengths, areas of competence and training needs in their induction year and thus help to programme their subsequent staff development. The TTA survey of the pilot project using these career entry profiles in 1996–97 has resulted in a short postponement of the intended September 1997 introduction but the TTA intends to rewrite the profiles, carry out a limited trial of them and introduce them for all new teachers as from 1998.

Before proceeding to examine and discuss the profiling of initial teacher training I will look at where the continuing professional development model based on recording of competences has come from.

Stages in the creation and design of Professional Development Profiles

a. Records of Achievement – recording, reflecting, target-setting

School leavers since 1992 have been compiling Records of Achievement to take to jobs and higher education as evidence of their work and achievements in secondary education over and beyond examination results (UCAS/SCUE, 1993).

There is some evidence that teacher trainers (under pressure to interview more candidates for fewer places because of changes in the clearing house procedures) spend little time examining RoAs and are more interested in examination results and personality displayed in the interview. One university professor reported to me that the most likely way in which they would respond to a candidate producing their RoA at interview would be to say, 'Tell me about the most significant achievements you have recorded and how they would contribute to your role as a teacher.' But he went on to add that no one would actually read through an RoA.

Despite this evidence of their lack of utility for employers at interview there is a strong belief in the profession that it is the process that is important even if the product has not yet achieved recognition. Perhaps because of this belief, there have been proposals that National Records of Achievement should be extended in their range and be established as 'a simple record of an individual's achievements throughout life which is nationally recognised' (Skinner, 1993).

Work by the Teacher Placement Service, in co-ordination with Leicester University, has examined the way in which these RoAs can be combined with individual action planning in initial teacher education to inform continuous professional development of teachers (Skinner, 1993). Examples of this work in the literature include Pritchard (1991), who discusses Records of Achievement as the means of providing profiles for trainee teachers. Fenwick and Nixon (1992a) and Fenwick, Assiter and Nixon (1992) in CNAA discussion papers look at the broader perspective of the identification and profiling of learning outcomes for students in HE at a time when the structure for awarding degrees changes to become more concerned with validating competences achieved and learning outcomes identified.

The Training Agency, the Department of the Environment and the National Council for Vocational Qualifications have long had an ambition to link all workplace-based learning (and who can deny that teacher training is increasingly becoming workplace-based) into a national scheme of NVQs based on competency. The Training Agency sponsored the 'Enterprise in HE' initiative which many higher education institutions (HEIs) have been involved in. Given that the NCVQ's objectives, which included 'providing opportunities for progression, including progression to higher education and professional qualifications' (NCVQ, 1986) are endorsed by the Department for Education and Employment there is little doubt that in future the records of achievement and competence for teachers will be clearly modelled on NCVQ principles.

b. Profiling development of competences in initial teacher training – stage one profiles

Although there has long been an interest in setting up and maintaining records of development across the three stages of teacher education it is only recently that this has led to the concept of profiling progress in a professional portfolio (Mortimore, 1990; Whitty and Willmott, 1991; Pritchard, 1987; Davies, 1993; Wall and Smith, 1993; Tomlinson and Saunders, 1994; Broadfoot, 1994).

Particular interest has been shown in the way in which students can map their own development through reflection on their experience. Anglia Polytechnic University has explored this concept with their primary B.Ed. students, basing its methods on Schön (1987) and Pollard and Tann (1993). Profiles which include planning and target-setting for their next stage of development by students with their tutors have also featured in many schemes (e.g. Crewe and Alsager, Homerton College, Roehampton Institute). In the latter two of these profiling schemes, students are required to produce evidence to tutors to justify their claims to competence in certain areas (such as classroom management or lesson preparation). In the Anglia Polytechnic University scheme, primary B.Ed. students are asked at regular intervals to reflect upon what they feel they have achieved in terms of understanding and mastering particular competences demanded by the course and then to set themselves targets for their next stage of learning. Secondary PGCE students at APU have been required to maintain a profile charting development in the TTA competences which acts as both a passport (requiring them to show it to each school they have experience in and to their tutor on each return to the university) and a 'road map' (setting out the direction of the course and alternative routes through it). This profile, though initially seen by many as daunting and time-consuming, has gained a good reputation with students because, as one student reported:

> At least you know where you are, how you are progressing in terms of the com-
> petences and, if your mentors and tutors can be persuaded to fill in their comments,
> you know what other people feel you need to focus on. It's better than getting to the
> end of the course and being told you've failed or need to do more work on one of the
> competences to pass.

Many academics have investigated the use of profiles in initial teacher training. For instance, Garrigan and Strivens (1991) examine the way in which records of professional development can become profiles which take on board the Secretary of State's competence criteria for secondary teachers (DES 24/89), and Pritchard (1987) examines the balance between formative and summative assessment of teaching practice and the way in which the school practice report is gradually becoming a kind of profile which he calls a record of professional achievement. When Pomeroy (1993) reviewed induction and mentor training courses by sending questionnaires to all HE training institutions in England and Wales he found that, of the 62 institutions which replied, 26 included the use of profiles referring to the needs of trainees and development of competences in their courses. The University of Warwick's PGCE secondary scheme includes a record of professional achieve-ment which can be used at later stages in the teacher's career for further professional development and as a link into appraisal schemes in schools.

Most profiles to date deal only with the general competences of teaching and are derived from a combination of earlier teaching practice report forms and the 9/92 or 14/93 competences. Although in every case that I have examined there has been one section on subject knowledge, few HEIs have subdivided this into levels. Exceptions to this have been Bedford (de Montford University) and the University of East Anglia, who discussed their attempts to produce 'level statements' for subject knowledge at an ERTEC conference in 1994. The DFE in AM 14/93 proposed three levels of subject knowledge competence for primary teachers:

Level 1: 'the basic familiarity with a subject that can be reasonably expected of a
       newly qualified teacher';
Level 2: 'enhanced subject competence ... stronger sense of concepts and method-
       ology ... independent professional judgements can be made ...
       Induction/in-service support is necessary';

Level 3: 'insight into structures, concepts content and principles of a subject ... autonomy over approaches and resources ... capable of providing real professional leadership.

These level statements were thought to be the way the TTA was going with its career entry profiles, but concerted rejection by the Universities and Colleges of Education of Teachers (UCET) and the teacher unions led to the abandonment of levels and their replacement with the categories of strength, competence and need for development.

This profiling of progress towards achievement of the competences by trainee teachers as recorded in the career entry profile will inform planning by schools and local education authorities of their induction programmes for newly qualified teachers. The whole process of profiling of competence, however, has many dilemmas attached and we would like to look at some of them before moving on to see how profiling initial competence can link with induction and continuing professional development.

The key question seems to be: How do you measure a teacher's competence and what does a competent teacher look like? This is of course the question that has been at the forefront of debate in teacher education for many years. What constitutes a pass on teaching practice, and what is a competent teacher? We continue to read the debate in the newspapers about incompetent teachers and the need to get rid of them. (Even Michael Barber, Labour leader Tony Blair's guru on education, would like to see 'poor teachers' removed by a General Teachers Council – *Guardian*, 22.10.96.) There are teachers in schools whose lessons are defined by OFSTED as unsatisfactory and head teacher and governors are being informed of their performance. But they are qualified; therefore, in terms of the TTA, accepted competent. So the question becomes, are they incompetent or was it merely a poor performance on the day, or is the context in which they are teaching inappropriate for their knowledge and experience (one of the key factors in poor performance identified in *The New Teacher in School 1992* (OFSTED, 1993b), which we discuss later in this chapter)? Perhaps most importantly for the future of education is the question of what can be done about apparently incompetent teachers. How can we use professional profiling to ensure that continuing teacher development improves lessons, teaching and learning?

Sam Saunders at Leeds University conducted a national survey of ITT profiling and touched on some of the problems in his letter to contributing HEIs. On the problem of defining the competent teacher he proposed that the aim is to produce:

> *a competent beginning teacher*, which we can take to mean adequately competent to be entrusted with the duties of a qualified teacher, including being entrusted with planning, preparing, managing and assessing the learning of average ... students.

On quality control and the problems of context he suggests: 'it is a judgement of capability requiring evidence that they can achieve that aspect relatively *consistently* (i.e. have done so on a number of occasions) and *intelligently* (i.e. demonstrating insight into what they are doing' (Tomlinson and Saunders, 1994).

The big question schools will want answered, in order to meet parental demands for school improvement and in order to achieve OFSTED criteria, is: Can profiling linked to appraisal and staff development help to solve the problem of linking entry requirements to continuing competence and further professional development?

So what is a competent teacher?

I offer here a summary of what teacher trainers and OFSTED seem to have in common in defining competence. The debate about what is a good teacher has been pursued in the journals and we would particularly recommend the work of Professor Edgar Stones in that area. I offer a list of those qualities of what seem to me to be the present defining characteristics. Thus a competent teacher is one who:

- is professionally committed to promoting the education and well-being of all children regardless of their cultural, ethnic or religious backgrounds;
- knows their specialist subject or curriculum area well enough to teach it and inform less knowledgeable colleagues on what and how to teach in that subject;
- can teach the key ideas and content of their subject in a variety of ways which meet the learning styles of different ability and interest groups;
- can manage children in a quiet and ordered manner in and out of the class-room;
- can work equably with children, colleagues, parents, governors and administrators;
- can relate to children as individuals and develop their interest in learning;
- encourages the spiritual, moral, social and cultural development of children;
- is committed to the idea of lifetime professional development for the sake of their students, their school and themselves; and
- can accept the need for continuous change in order to meet the needs of their clients and employers.

It is obvious from this list of criteria that the person I define (as a result of taking on board both OFSTED definitions of competence and a wider view of the competent professional) goes beyond the competences listed in DfEE publications. This list therefore has implications for the design of profiles with a broader range of competences needed to be a competent professional.

Having explored the definition of a competent teacher at the beginner stage I will look at the use of profiles in the induction year. However, I further examine the way in which profiles can be designed to cover broader professional development at the end of this chapter.

Profiling development in the induction year

Government, through HMI, has expressed the need for closer links between higher education and local education authorities in recent years (with particular emphasis on maximizing the impact of induction by ensuring that it met the individual needs of new teachers). In *The Induction and Probation of New Teachers 1988–1991* (DES, 1992b) Her Majesty's Inspectors make the point that:

> Agreement on what professional skills need to be acquired by new teachers by the end of their first year of teaching would greatly help schools and LEAs plan their support. Teacher training institutions can help by clearly identifying the skills possessed by their students who have just been awarded qualified teacher status. (DES, 1992b, p. 1)

This clearly pointed to the need for a detailed individualized professional exit profile to inform employers of strengths and future training needs. The TTA career entry profile is designed to meet this need. It is worth noting that the career entry profile is linked to the new TTA monitoring of HEI quality in that it identifies the training institution of the newly qualified teacher. OFSTED, in its inspection of schools, also reports back on the quality of newly qualified teachers according to their training institution.

In general, the opinion of teachers is broadly in favour of some form of profiling though there has been much reaction to the concept of competences (e.g., Norris, 1991; Thompson, 1991; Carr, 1993; Calderhead, 1994; Furlong, 1994). Earley (1992), in his survey of local authority input into induction for newly qualified teachers, found that 77 per cent of his respondents favoured a nationally agreed profile of skills or competences for NQTs on completion of training, and 78 per cent agreed that this should be updated at the end of their first year in post. 'It was suggested that this profile of skills or competences should be devised by the profession itself. LEAs, schools, ITT institutions and professional associations all had a role to play' (Earley, 1992, p. 17). Earley's view of how the profile should be compiled underestimated the power of Her Majesty's Chief Inspector, the Teacher Training Agency and the government's right-wing think-tanks. The profile was produced, interested parties were given one month – August – to comment and it was then distributed for its pilot. The only change that resulted from the consultation exercise was that levels were abandoned and replaced with descriptions of competence, strengths or developmental needs.

So, after many years of identified need, the profession now has a career entry profile to help schools to provide effective induction and further training for newly qualified teachers. The question to address now is: 'Will the existence of the career entry profile bring about the desired improvements in professional competence and development?'

The New Teacher in School 1992 (OFSTED, 1993b) spoke of the need to link induction programmes with previous ITT experience and went on to say: 'There was no evidence, however, of student profiles from initial training being used by schools or LEAs to identify their [NQTs'] current training needs or to assist in the planning of induction programmes' (p. 35). As we will see later in this chapter the biggest problem in profiling is not producing the profiles but in convincing all concerned to use them and to see them as valuable sources of records of achievement and developmental targets rather than as just another administrative chore.

There is one more issue which it is worth raising before proceeding to examine the role of profiles of induction and that is to ask what part context plays in the achievement of competence. OFSTED, in *The New Teacher in School 1992* (OFSTED, 1993b), reported that some new teachers were given inappropriate placements and had unrealistic demands made upon them. Teachers who begin their career in a class which is in a well-managed suburban school have a distinct advantage over those who are placed in more disadvantaged inner-city schools with less strong management. The standards of the head of an LMS school with powerful parents and governors may be much higher than those that the head of a struggling inner-city school can afford to espouse – thus a new teacher at the former may be given less help and sympathy than one at the latter. John Furlong expressed a cogent critique in his paper at the 1994 British Education Research Association at Oxford when he declared: 'The ... weakness ... of any national system based on competences is that such instruments imply a decontextualized view of performance. But performance is not only multi-faceted, it is dependent on context' (p. 5). It is worth remembering that teacher success in the induction year (or during an OFSTED inspection) may rely on context as much as competence.

Profiling induction – stage two in professional profiling

It is clear that the final section of the career entry profile which identifies the training and development requirements of the newly qualified teacher will become the first section of their induction profile. Thus it is worth asking what an induction profile should look like and what it should record.

If competence is the level which should be attained in order to pass a teacher training course, what is the next stage of development, that which newly qualified teachers should be aiming for? Eraut (1989) addressed this issue in an interesting way in an article in which he was discussing whether NVQs had any relevance in teacher education programmes using a version of Dreyfus' description of skill acquisition (Dreyfus and Dreyfus, 1984) as adapted by Benner (1982).

Summary of the Dreyfus model of skills acquisition

LEVEL I

Novice

Rigid adherence to taught rules or plans

Little situational perception

No discretionary judgement

LEVEL 2

Advanced beginner

Guidelines for action based on attributes or aspects (aspects are global characteristics of situations recognizable only after some prior experience)

Situational perception still limited

All attributes and aspects are treated separately and given equal importance

LEVEL 3

Competence

Coping with crowdedness

Now sees actions at least partially in terms of longer-term goals

Conscious deliberate planning

Standardized and routinized procedures

LEVEL 4

Proficient

Sees situations holistically rather than in terms of aspects

Sees what is most important in a situation

Perceives deviations from the normal pattern

Decision-making less laboured

Uses maxims for guidance, whose meaning varies according to the situation

LEVEL 5

Expert

No longer relies on rules, guidelines or maxims

Intuitive grasp of situations based on deep tacit understanding

Analytic approaches used only in novel situations or when problems occur

Vision of what is possible

Eraut, in discussing the model, focuses on the 'significant qualitative gap between the competent and the proficient'. He goes on to define this:

> Competency is the climax of rule guided learning and discovering how to cope in crowded, pressured contexts, whereas proficiency marks the onset of quite a different approach to the job. Normal behaviour is not just routinised but semi-automatic. Situations are apprehended more deeply and the abnormal is quickly spotted and given attention. The sense of priority is clear and strategic approaches are used. However, more experience of successful problem solving and strategic planning is needed before expertise can be said to have developed. (p. 183)

There seems to be here a tension between an organization's responsibility for ensuring continuous training and development for its staff and each individual's need for self-evaluation, development, growth and change in their careers. The first perspective is present in staff training days (what schools still call Baker days) and induction courses. The second is represented by the in-service courses, which both local education authorities and universities run, and the other learning extension which employees undertake, including Open University courses and conference attendance.

Such initiatives as Investors in People are important in encouraging employers to provide training opportunities for employees. In order to obtain IIP recognition employers must provide a cycle of development which includes: a continuing commitment to investing in people; planning to meet people's skills needs; actioning the plan; and evaluating the result to repeat the cycle and increase the effect.

There is a need for professional portfolios for career teachers, on the same basis that trainees and inductees need profiles, in order that recording of training and development undertaken is matched with reflection on the experiences in both a formative and summative manner. The portfolio provides the basis for teachers to ask the key linked questions 'What have I achieved?' and 'What must I do now I've reached this stage in my personal development?' In a school committed to improving its performance for the sake of its students, teachers' individual developmental needs will be recognized and met, with priority being given to those which match institutional development plans.

Research implications for the design of induction programmes and portfolios

My research into induction processes and practices in five LEAs (Turner, 1992) provides some suggestions which could inform the setting up of a system of induction profiles and career-long professional development portfolios. For the sake of this discussion I highlight three key issues, discuss them, and update the implications of the findings, before going on to look at the way in which one LEA designed an induction portfolio.

Research findings

1. The research revealed *the importance of LEAs getting their administrative procedures for probation and induction working effectively*; for these policies to be clearly communicated to all involved; for systems to be evaluated to ensure they were working efficiently and to establish that there were effective working relationships between all participants.

2. Most interviewees suggested *changes in LEA centre-based induction courses* so that they will:

a. deliver information, techniques and ideas in the most effective order for new teachers;
b. attempt to meet more effectively the individual needs of new teachers (e.g. infant, junior or secondary; B.Ed. or PGCE; trained in England and Wales or overseas); and
c. complement more effectively initial training and ongoing school-based teacher development.

3. Many interviewees in management posts (heads, advisers and inspectors) spoke of the *importance of seeing teacher education as an ongoing process* and of wanting to build more effective links between initial teacher training institutions, LEAs and schools involved in induction programmes, school-based staff development, in-service provision and higher education courses – ensuring broader teacher involvement and giving credit for courses attended.

Discussion

Now that probation has been abolished there is still a clear need for LEAs and locally managed schools to ensure that they keep a clear record of:

* where NQTs are placed;
* whether they are receiving an induction programme;
* the way in which they are helped to develop;
* whether they are being monitored and assessed to ascertain their competence.

This information is important since employers of newly qualified teachers need clear information about their suitability and competence before renewing their contracts at the end of the induction year. Not only is proper induction necessary to improve schools and ensure maximized learning by pupils, but it is an essential audit of human resource management and professional development processes. Teacher recruitment and induction is an expensive process and local authorities and schools where teacher turnover is high suffer not only from increased human resource expenses but more importantly from a lack of continuity which can damage the education of the children.

Since the research was conducted, most local education authorities have undergone major changes in the way in which their in-service programmes for teachers, including induction courses, are organized. The new LEA teams are more concerned to meet the espoused needs of their clients, the teachers and their schools, than to offer a broad-ranging programme. Often the LEA programmes are affected by DfEE directed funding (GEST grants) which are designated for particular areas. In 1992 and 1993, induction was one of these areas and it was for this reason that many LEAs set up pilot schemes to develop induction profiles and portfolios. Nevertheless, research reveals that LEAs are still not always meeting the needs of schools and this is particularly true with induction of newly qualified teachers where there is a tension between the need to plan ahead and the problem of not knowing the espoused needs of newly qualified teachers until the September when they actually arrive in the schools which the LEA services. Perhaps early analysis of new teachers' career entry profiles will provide a data base for the planning of induction training provision in future?

The third area – that of seeing teacher education as an ongoing process – has been one in which much progress has been made. Many LEAs are working more closely with the HE training institutions in the designing and teaching of induction and the training of school-based mentors. The newly qualified teachers and their mentors are often being offered accreditation for the work they do in the induction year and induction portfolios are often the basis of their being offered this accreditation by the universities.

LEA induction profiles

One LEA, Essex County Council, introduced the idea of professional profiles (EDAS, 1992) for new teachers in order to structure development in the induction year. These portfolios were designed by a joint working party between Essex Education Development and Advisory Service and four universities (Anglia Polytechnic University; Brighton University; Greenwich University and Homerton College, Cambridge University). These portfolios were piloted, revised, launched on a county-wide basis, evaluated and redesigned.

Research findings

When the evaluation team asked users for their views, the portfolios were generally seen as well designed and useful for their purpose of supporting NQTs and mentors in the induction year. However, the evaluation team recommended the following steps to further improve the effectiveness of the portfolios:

i.   timely introduction of the materials to schools for early use by Heads, mentors and NQTs

ii.   enhancing the use of the portfolios by mentors and NQTs

iii. enabling NQTs to benefit from the critical reflections and support provided by well-trained and competent mentors

iv.   continuous evaluation by EDAS of the implementation of the materials and subsequent staff development. (Maude and Turner, 1993)

Discussion

The research revealed that too often the induction portfolios did not arrive in schools before term began and thus were left behind in the tide of events which the NQT and their mentor dealt with as they happened. Often, too, the portfolios had arrived in the school but had been filed or shelved by a senior manager, and the mentor and NQT did not get to use them. Where mentors and NQTs had received the portfolios early, either before term began or at the beginning of term, they usually built them into the induction programme and found them a useful way of structuring their work over the induction year.

Training for mentors in how to carry out induction development for NQTs and for NQTs on how to cope with the induction year was also significant. It was particularly important for both parties to have been introduced to the portfolio and to have been shown how to use it incrementally rather than receiving the large and daunting document on the first day of term and being put off by it. Where training had been undertaken, both mentors and NQTs were more likely to use and benefit from the materials in the induction portfolio. Training too was likely to enable mentors to be confident in modelling reflection and helping NQTs to develop as reflective practitioners.

The LEA was very committed to learning from the evaluation and immediately undertook measures to ensure improvements in the portfolio, better and earlier distribution, and greater encouragement of mentors and NQTs to attend training in using the portfolios.

Other LEAs, including Enfield (Goddard, 1993), Barking and Dagenham, Newham and Surrey (Gifford, 1992), have introduced the concept of professional profiles or portfolios for their staff, from NQTs through to whole-career development. There is evidence in Earley (1994) that a number of LEAs have been using profiles and portfolios since 1992 to keep track of NQTs' professional development. In Earley's sample of six LEAs the following pattern emerged:

> Two shire counties had developed and were using competence-based profiles; a metropolitan borough had devised and piloted separate portfolios for its primary and secondary NQTs; a London borough had used a pre-appointment personal profile to identify the main components of NQTs' training along with their strengths and areas for further development. (p. 112)

Some schools have designed their own competency schemes for inducting and training both initial trainees and NQTs. One of the better known of these was edited by Mike Berrill (1991). Berrill, of Challney Community College, listed twelve teacher competences with five levels of achievement – *Not Evident, Elementary, Growing Competence, Basic Proficiency* and *Well Developed* – which he built into a teacher profile for use in an induction programme. Each competence has space for a determination of levels linked to setting targets for development and mentor action.

Summary – induction profiles and portfolios

If the recording of competences and their link to professional development is to be successful in schools it will be necessary to ensure that profiles are:

- high on management's agenda;
- derived from discussion between all those with a stake in individual and school development;
- the source of targets for future individual development as well as a record of achievement; and
- recognized as an important aspect of school development and improvement.

As we have noted above, the TTA career entry profile will influence the design of induction profiles and continuing professional development portfolios because it will effectively lay down the structure of the opening section. There are clearly advantages in common practice which will enable teachers who move around the country to use their profiles and portfolios more effectively to gain employment and to gain credit for their experience when registering for further professional qualifications. Universities are increasingly asking teachers to produce evidence of prior attainment and experience in portfolio form when they register for advanced diplomas and master's degrees (accreditation of prior learning and accreditation of prior experience) in order to give them credit modules on their programmes.

One application of the accreditation scheme is to encourage teachers in their induction year to keep a record of their progress through the induction year which they can submit to their local authority or the validating university for accreditation. First-year teachers who use the induction profile to provide them with a structure for keeping notes on their progress through the year can then submit a portfolio together with a reflective summary of their year's learning and progress and some ideas of targets for the future as a portfolio for accreditation. This system has the dual advantage of setting a target for the induction year which gives new teachers a clear pathway to follow and of starting them on a lifetime programme of continuing professional development. The Credit Accumulation and Transfer (CATS) points they gain can have the effect of encouraging them to go on to further study and higher qualifications.

In-service: continuing professional development – stage three profiles

In the past, in-service for teachers has been an uncoordinated mixture of inputs from school-based training days, through LEA day-release and twilight courses to university-validated higher awards. Many teachers who followed award-bearing courses in the past did so by gaining a period of secondment. This process has almost entirely disappeared and teachers are now having to study in their own time. This has led universities to provide shorter, more fragmented courses composed of modules which can be built up over a period of time to achieve a higher qualification such as an advanced diploma or MA.

Access courses introduced teacher educators to the idea of alternative ways of accrediting teachers' prior learning – often by the system of compiling portfolios of study and work experience. These courses were designed to encourage teachers who did not have the traditionally necessary good honours degree to register for advanced diplomas and master's degrees. Anglia Polytechnic University (then Essex Institute of HE), together with North East London Polytechnic, was amongst the pioneers of the application of this system of Accreditation of Prior Learning (APL) and Accreditation of Prior Experiential Learning (APEL) to in-service for teachers (Winter and Powney, 1988). In place of formal entry requirements for the M.Ed. degree, teachers were given tutorial guidance in preparing:

> a portfolio of work which documents possession of a level of professional knowledge and awareness equivalent to that represented by a B.Ed. Hons qualification ... [which] encourages students to use their own educational and professional experiences to meet the criteria of assessment of a course which is a pre-requisite for entry to the M.Ed. (pp. 55–6)

The same process of credit accumulation has led to greater recognition of the role of school- and LEA-based courses as part of teachers' professional development.

In one particularly interesting case a whole school took on APL and APEL as part of an INSET policy designed to bring about school improvement and involve more teachers in professional development. The school, in partnership with APU, arranged courses on training days, in the evenings, at weekends and in holiday periods based at the school or at convenient local venues in order to encourage staff to take part. They paid teachers' fees and provided a staff development officer to encourage participation. This is a very successful scheme with high staff take-up and a clear programme linked to school development needs as well as providing individuals with career development options. It is monitored and moderated by the university, which accredits the modules and provides tutors for research method modules and the final dissertation modules of the master's degree course.

The accreditation of prior learning approach has been employed by many higher education institutions both at M.Ed. level and for the gradual accumulation of credit towards certificates and diplomas, often in co-operation with LEA in-service provision. Examples include Surrey and the West London boroughs' co-operation with the South West London Teacher Education Council and the Thames Regional In-Service Network which had a team responsible for 'developing a Professional Profile for staff who are new to teaching or for Accreditation of Prior Learning reflecting on their previous five years' experience'. Recently, Anglia Polytechnic University has developed partnership arrangements with Essex LEA and Suffolk LEA – agreeing to accredit LEA-run courses as part of the modular INSET scheme, thus enabling teachers to gain credit for school-based INSET and local education authority courses they attend towards university-validated awards.

Practical concerns

One important question about the professional profile concerns how it would work. Who would have ownership and rights of access and what validity would it have? This question takes on a particular poignancy in the light of the changing nature of post qualification learning for teachers from Baker Days, through LEA courses, HEI INSET and privately run conferences and courses.

We would suggest that the portfolio is the property of the teacher from the point of qualification. However, extracts from the portfolio would need to be summarized and certified, or validated, by a recognized senior colleague or manager (such as a mentor, staff development tutor, head of department or head teacher) whenever they are to be used as evidence. These summaries or extracts may be used, for instance, at appraisal interviews, at internal promotion boards, as part of an application for another post, or as evidence for APL in joining an HEI INSET programme. It is unlikely that future employers or interview panels will want to review a whole portfolio or profile before an appointment is made.

It is useful here to establish what might count as evidence of competence in a profile or portfolio. This is a difficult area and in order to answer it let us take one example – competence in classroom control or management. In order for this to be stated confidently, it seems to us that there would need to be signed statements (appraisal or mentoring reports) from at least two people, citing lessons observed and giving contextual support to the claim. It would not be good enough for the teachers themselves to claim that they could control the class nor would the evidence suffice of someone who had not watched them teach but claimed 'the class always seemed to be working all right when I looked in' (the words of one head, reporting on how he completed the induction year report). Professional profiles demand professional evidence.

Another difficulty which the induction profile has to overcome is the broad nature of the competences. Perhaps we have lessons to learn from NVQs and the ASSET programme in designing our profiles – i.e., each competence would be broken down into sub-statements. Thus teachers who wish to claim that they have achieved competence would be expected to produce evidence supporting each sub-statement to an assessor. This evidence will only be useful and relevant when it is generally recognized that the portfolio has status and is part of recognized staff development. This works with NVQs, the ASSET programme and the Management Charter Initiative, for instance. Thus the process of profiling will only be effective when it is recognized as professionally necessary.

What kinds of professional development would teachers record in their portfolio?

Not everybody wants promotion or more responsibility. Many good teachers enjoy their job so much that they do not want to become managers, 'stuck in offices doing administration' and away from the classroom. Others are quite clear that they have ambition and vision and that they want to 'run their own school' and to influence policy in education. A few feel that they want to pass on what they have learned through becoming teacher trainers or advisers.

We would like to suggest three routes which teachers could follow, which HEIs, LEAs and others could provide for and which professional profiles could be designed to accommodate.

Professional maintenance

Here a teacher undertakes sufficient training and development to maintain an up-to-date and professional standard but wishes to retain their present role. This route would satisfy government and school demands for evidence of development in essential areas but would allow classroom teachers to focus on their subject expertise, classroom management and the needs of their pupils without pressure to take on further responsibilities in the school. This might be the route for mid-career teachers with no ambition for promotion and no desire to take on further responsibility.

Expert teacher

This refers to a professional development process which enables a teacher to remain in the classroom but to become a source of expertise to other colleagues – especially trainees, new teachers and staff who are in need of particular development and training. This teacher might well be the school mentor or staff development tutor. The development for this teacher might be in specialist subject knowledge, in learning theory – including understanding how adults learn – in counselling and in theories of pedagogy and classroom management. Perhaps they would move on to university or LEA work or become the school Staff Development Officer.

Management in education

This would be a professional development route which would lead from subject or pastoral responsibility on to middle and then senior management. This route might be informed by the Management Charter Initiative standards. This route, though inevitably moving the teacher away from the classroom to some extent, would still demand elements of professional maintenance. Further professional development might include understanding organizations, curriculum development, personnel management, time management, pastoral, health and safety, or site management.

The future of professional development for teachers

We have already suggested that it is government's intention to press for continuous professional development across all employment, including the professions and especially in the caring professions. In professions with a general council or ruling body such as medicine, engineering and architecture there has been a move to insist on individuals maintaining professional development if they are to retain membership. In some states of the United States teachers are expected to show evidence of continuing professional development up to MA level if they wish to retain tenure. The proposed General Teaching Council is suggesting that teachers should have a five-year 'MOT' on their effectiveness and that they should be expected to keep evidence of their continuing professional development in order to maintain professional registration (Barber, 1995).

Perhaps a system of professional portfolios will enable teachers to:

a. demonstrate, by recording attendance at courses and conferences and training days, that they are continuing their professional development;
b. develop an awareness of their own and the school's needs and by further study and reflection continue to improve both their own performance, the institution's effectiveness and the quality of children's learning.

INSET has changed a great deal over the past five years and has developed a scheme for continuing professional development of teachers based on recording learning of both the award-bearing and experiential kinds. Other professions have been following similar patterns and it is worth looking at one of them to compare how education measures up to other schemes.

Competence profiling and the ASSET programme

One of the more interesting developments in professional development schemes in recent years has been the post-qualification development in social work and nursing which has been a competence-based scheme – the ASSET programme (Winter and Maisch, 1991; Probert, Maisch and Winter, 1992). The way in which this has been introduced may have direct implications for future teacher professional development. Based on experience with NVQs – with the emphasis on achieving demonstrable workplace qualities and skills – the programme calls for competence statements to be backed by evidence produced by the student and supported by a supervisor or tutor.

The development programme set out to define a core set of skills for each professional role by asking key professionals what they did and creating a bank of competences. (This is quite clearly more professional than the early DFE and CATE approach.) These competences were grouped into modules which post-qualification professionals could attain by collecting evidence for each listed element of competence, supported by a supervisor, or claim accreditation of prior learning by submitting portfolios of evidence. Where they felt a need to acquire new skills or competences they could register for courses or indicate areas of learning they would like to undertake with tutor and/or supervisor support. Assessors are appointed to help supervisors ensure that students' evidence is of an acceptable standard. It is worth noting here, however, that the biggest difference between this scheme and the TTA-developed teacher one is that the competences were developed from the espoused and observed competences of leading professionals. Particularly interesting, and absent from the teacher competences, is their overarching and prerequisite criterion (or competence) 'Commitment to Professional Values'.

Criterion No 1: Commitment to Professional Values

Demonstrates self-awareness and commitment in implementing professional values in practice.
This involves demonstrating:

1. the ability to understand and to implement anti-discriminatory, anti-oppressive and anti-racist principles;
2. awareness of the need to counteract one's own tendency (both as a person and as a professional worker endowed with specific powers) to behave oppressively;
3. respect for client's dignity, privacy, autonomy and rights as service users;
4. ability to manage complex ethical responsibilities and value conflicts;
5. ability to empower others. (Probert, Maisch and Winter, 1992, p. 29)

Would these not equally apply to teachers? Why does the Teacher Training Agency not consider this area as important? Is the achievement of competence in observed performance all that is required? Perhaps the much vaunted General

Teachers Council, at present waiting in the wings for full union and government approval, would be able to set an agenda for teacher qualification at initial, induction and further levels. If the GTC takes control of the profession in the way that doctors' and lawyers', architects' and engineers' professional associations and councils have, teachers in future might see a greater focus on professional development.

Conclusion

The challenge to designers of professional development portfolios – which might include teacher profiles – is to find a format which will be helpful, informative and acceptable to the users. Whilst many teachers are committed to ongoing professional development they are also extremely busy – the research by Jim Campbell at Warwick has revealed an enormous increase in the hours teachers work since the Education Reform Act. Heads and other potential audiences for the portfolio are not only very busy, they have become sceptical about files and portfolios. Therefore the system we design needs to lend itself to a low-maintenance but regularly reviewed document which has the facility for providing extracts and summaries for a variety of purposes as well as providing more detailed records and reflective material.

I conclude the chapter with a first broad attempt to outline what the contents of a professional profile might be.

Career-long professional profile for teachers

Stage 1. Initial teacher training – achievement of competence

a. from school to HE – records of achievement;
b. professional portfolios – recording activities and achievements, reflecting on successes and problems, target setting for future training and development (individual action planning), profiling development of competences – evidence plus supervisor's comments;
c. exit profile/career entry profile – clear record of levels of experiences and levels of achievement in initial training based on TTA competences plus some contextualization, targets for further development and proposed areas of specialism.

(The Teacher Training Authority pilot Career Entry Profile was published in 1996, trialled in 1996–7 and is being revised, re-trialled ready for use with all teachers in 1997–8 (McPake et al., 1997).)

Stage 2. Induction year – post-qualification record of achievement

a. record of induction experiences and training both in school and on external courses;
b. record and celebration of particular skills, talents and contributions to school and community;
c. target-setting for competences needing development (transferred from Career Entry Profile) or areas demanding special attention in first appointment;
d. revisiting competence statements to ensure maintenance and development – end-of-year review;
e. end-of-year planning for future professional development and future specialism within school, with links to future appraisal or career development processes.

Stage 3. In-service – portfolio of ongoing professional development

a. record of professional development both in school and on external courses – useful for curriculum vitae, credit accumulation (APEL and APL) purposes and for supporting appraisal;
b. revisiting competence statements to ensure maintenance and development – review progress and set targets in yearly appraisal;
c. reference to school development plans and individual target-setting for professional development or areas needing special attention in the school in future;
d. planning for further professional development and future role within school or in next job;
e. professional 'passport' recognized by employers and General Teaching Council.

Chapter 9

Pulling It All Together: Professional Development Schools

Mike Turner

In this chapter I look at the way in which the various aspects of change and improvement in schools can be linked to create a system for school improvement which achieves more than a simple aggregation of the parts. To this end I examine the literature on school improvement and professional development schools and discuss ways in which the research can inform today's schools. I also share ideas and insights from a tour of North American schools and universities I undertook with the intention of examining the way in which the mentor or 'master teacher' can contribute to teacher training in professional development schools and school/university partnerships.

There is little doubt that most of the latest international initiatives in education – raising of students' standards of attainment, a concern with school improvement, changes in the initial training of teachers, continuing professional development and the action research movement – are interconnected. One way in which educationalists have made sense of this interconnectedness is through the setting up of school/university partnerships.

The best of these partnerships are negotiated and democratic working agreements which offer opportunities and benefits to all concerned (Wayne, 1985; Furlong et al., 1988; Booth, Furlong and Wilkin, 1990; Shaw, 1992; Greenes, 1994; Sears, 1994; Bines and Welton, 1995). Perhaps the ultimate working out of partnerships has been in the creation of networks of professional development schools linked to universities. These kinds of partnerships are in their early stages in some parts of England but there is a longer history of experimentation with the process in the United States and recently much evidence of success (Brainard, 1989; Stallings and Kowalski, 1990; Boles, 1994; Zeichner, 1995; Bullough et al. 1996; Myers, 1996; Teitel, 1994 and 1996).

Let us begin by defining professional development schools (PDSs). Linda Darling-Hammond, one of the leading authorities on this subject, describes how

PDSs are different from previous initiatives:

> PDSs aim to provide new models of teacher education and development by serving as exemplars of practice, builders of knowledge and vehicles for the communication of professional understandings among teacher educators, novices and veteran teachers. They support the learning of prospective and beginning teachers by creating settings in which novices enter professional practice by working with expert practitioners, enabling veteran teachers to renew their own professional development and assume new roles as mentors, university adjuncts, and teacher leaders. They allow school and university educators to engage jointly in research and rethinking of practice, thus creating an opportunity for the profession to expand its knowledge base by putting research into practice – and practice into research. (Darling-Hammond, 1994, p. 1)

The ideal professional development school working in partnership with university teacher educators would provide a base for the early professional training and education of entrants to the profession. The trainees would be attached to the school as interns or associate teachers. This would mean that the teacher would be acting as a trainer/mentor/model (co-operating teacher is the most common title for these supervisors in the US) for the trainees and would perforce need to reflect on their own practice and theoretical position in the course of working with their mentee. In many cases it would mean that the teacher would come into contact with the university in several ways: through their induction and training in the role of mentor; through regular meetings with the visiting university tutor (or university adjunct); through helping trainees to make sense of their theoretical lectures in practical classroom situations, and possibly through the contacts involved in undertaking action research to qualify for the in-service module offered by many universities to its co-operating teachers.

At the same time, administrators in the district and the school would be aware of the opportunities for joint research with the university offered by the presence of students and a supervising academic in their school, an opportunity sometimes made possible by the finance which the university makes available as a *quid pro quo* for their taking on teacher training supervision. In many cases students will undertake research projects which are important for the school, and in a few cases the professor, the teacher and the students will jointly examine a problem or issue as part of an action research network (see Zeichner, 1992). Similarly the university can benefit from employing the teachers to contribute to practical classroom courses and to exploit their newly revitalized interest in theory by asking them to contribute to university theory-based courses.

The core objective of any school is to improve the learning and achievements of its students and any other activities which the school is involved in must not be allowed to interfere with that. Schools are under enormous pressures to produce better results for less funding across broader ranges of subjects. Obviously some of these pressures are external and, in England, come from government and other national bodies, such as the Office for Standards in Education (OFSTED), the Teacher Training Authority (TTA) and the pronouncements of the political parties and their 'think-tanks'. In the United States, where similar pressures have been around for many years, the Holmes group (1986, 1990), the Carnegie Forum on Education and the Economy (1986), and more recently the National Committee for Accreditation of Teacher Training all see placement in professional development schools as a key aspect of trainee teachers' development and consequently of school improvement.

Various independent initiatives are also aiming to bring about change in England and the United States: the school improvement movement (associated with Wideen and Andrews (1987), Fullan (1992), Hargreaves (1994) and Hopkins (1994)) has been pro-active in seeking to build from within schools. More recently work has focused on what school children can tell us about school improvement (Ruddock, 1995), the role of inspection in school improvement (Earley, 1997), research's input to school improvement (Gray, 1996), and how strategic planning can help bring about improvement (Fidler, 1996). At the same time a surge of interest in the British Standard award Investors in People has led to an interest in demonstrating that schools have a sound professional development policy which is one clear route to developing and improving schools.

Teachers are the key to school improvement. Schools rely on teachers to plan, teach and assess learning, so PDSs need to have clear recruitment, induction and staff development policies. In order that staff recruitment, induction and continuing professional development can be effective there needs to be clear policies and a senior member of staff responsible. Professional development and school improvement policies need to be publicized to all staff and supported by the senior management team. In the United States this concept has been embraced by some school districts by the appointment of master teachers (though this title is not much loved by fellow teachers) to pro-active development roles in schools. In England there is a move by the Teacher Training Authority to promote the concept of the 'chartered' or 'expert' teacher as a leading professional who will undertake responsibility for training and professional development work rather than progressing to head of department or head teacher roles.

Professional development schools – research tour of North America

When, in 1995, I had the opportunity to bid for research funding, as part of the Research Funding Council's attempts to enable new universities' opportunities to expand their research base, I decided that it was the concept of the master teacher or expert teacher as the pivotal figure in continuing professional development that I wanted to examine. Because I had looked at the growing research coming in from the United States on the concept of continuing professional development as part of the professional development schools movement, it was to this issue that I directed my attention.

The aim of the research tour was to discover how universities on the other side of the Atlantic were approaching partnership with schools and to what extent the role of the classroom teacher was developing into a mentoring/professional development/master teacher position within their schools. The idea for the research developed from a visit to Anglia Polytechnic University by Dorothy Lloyd from the San Marcos School of Education (a newly opened branch of the California State University, with whom APU had set up a sister university relationship).

In her address to our faculty, Dorothy Lloyd had spoken of the way in which co-operating teachers who acted as supervisors to trainee teachers within schools could go through a formal examination process and become master teachers who had both a relationship with the university as visiting professors and an enhanced role within their own schools as professional development advisers for their colleagues. This was so close to the ideas that we at APU were aiming at that it seemed a good idea to visit the university, interview the participants and assess to what extent it was working and how it might be applied to our own courses.

The opportunity to bid for research development funding led us to put in a wider ranging tour covering a variety of universities and concluding with a visit to the annual meeting of the American Education Research Association in order to get a broader perspective. After much frantic writing, telephoning and e-mailing we ended up with a very wide-ranging itinerary: starting in Southern California at San Marcos, moving on to Vancouver for the University of British Columbia and then on to the University of Wisconsin at Madison, concluding the research at Penn State, University of Pennsylvania, and going on to the AERA meeting in New York. These venues were chosen for a variety of reasons: San Marcos, California, because of Anglia's connections with them and their interest in new ways of training teachers; Madison because of Ken Zeichner, whose writing I knew and admired; University of British Columbia because I had read articles by Gaalen Ericson and heard him speak at AERA in New Orleans in 1994; and Penn State because it was one of the largest teacher training schools in the east (and with which I had a tentative contact).

In the course of this section I shall include extracts from my interviews and field notes but will concentrate on some of the important ideas and issues which arose at each of the universities. The core of the section will be a case study of one university's partnership with one school in an attempt to focus on key issues.

San Marcos, California State University

This was a bright new university still in the early stages of building, but with a well-developed school of education. I discovered that they had not developed the idea of master teachers and were not as concerned with the concept of mentoring as I had thought. They used co-operating teachers who undertook the supervision of their interns on school experience (the practicum), and some of these teachers contributed to the university-based programme. These co-operating teachers undertook a training programme at the university which gave them credits towards their master's degrees. Some university tutors were deeply committed to school-based work but many were more involved with university-based course delivery and research.

One key idea which I picked up at San Marcos, and which was much the same in all of the other universities, was that of the teaching practice co-ordinator and organizer being a seconded teacher. 'They are so much more successful than us at making connections with school teachers and principals – they know the language and use their networks', the head of the education faculty told me. The other striking difference from the situation in England was that the university super-vision visits to schools were mainly carried out by teacher fellows, university adjuncts. These teachers were usually seconded without pay for between one and three years to complete master's degrees or doctorates. Their work as an adjunct (supervisor) helped them to pay their tuition fees and to live during their study period. It was necessary to have a doctorate before becoming a member of faculty and some fellows stayed on when they got their doctorate and became associate professors.

It was the new associate professors who were most keenly interested in the development of new ideas in education and in the management of the practicum. The keenest of the associate professors worked regularly in schools providing support for their students and making input into the curriculum in their specialist area as part of the class teacher's professional development. I saw this in one elementary school where the visiting professor helped the mathematics teacher to run an after-school computer club for children, using the trainee teacher's skills to support them.

Perhaps the most interesting project that I saw that San Marcos was involved in was the way in which the arts were used to integrate and open up the curriculum in some schools. This co-operation was notably good in one junior high school which had a huge banner across the front of the school saying 'Recognized by the State as an Outstanding School'. It was at this school that two nine-year-old students interviewed me for the school television station in a most professional and incisive manner – they were especially interested in why English children had to wear school uniform.

Another school, which had been a run-down 'barrio' school from which pupils had been withdrawn at an alarming rate, was reformed as an arts academy and had become one of the most popular schools in the district with students bussed in from miles around. The idea was that the school, which was a combined elementary and junior high school, taught its whole curriculum through music, dance, drama and visual art. The university had contributed lecturer expertise in the arts and a steady stream of committed teacher education students to support the initiative. Whilst I was there one of the modules – on medieval English history – was assessed and the principal medium was a whole-group performance of a play about medieval England in which all students played roles which combined learning about history, the arts and politics of the time with the use of presentational form in all of the performing arts. It was an excellent production and the students clearly got a great deal out of it.

In another city centre the university had made a link between the Southern California Centre for the Performing Arts (a huge arts complex with two theatres, dance workshops, art galleries and a museum) and an elementary school such that performers and technicians from the arts complex visited the school and made an input into the children's learning, guided by a university professor and a group of trainee teachers using arts to explore the broader curriculum. In one classroom I saw one of the results, which was some stunning puppets, made by the children and used to present a play about the development of America and its Presidents (the Clinton puppet was especially good).

One high school (San Deguito Academy) provided a most dramatic example of how parent power and the will of the administration can bring about school improvement. Faced with becoming a local sink school because two new schools were being opened in their catchment area (the fastest growing population in the United States), the school council decided to make the school more attractive to parents and students. In order to establish a direction for this they wrote to 4,000 potential parents and students and asked for their views on what they would like to see in a revamped school. The answers were that parents and students wanted:

- to choose the principal – from the existing staff;
- all staff to re-apply for their jobs to a panel which included the new principal, the chair of the parents association and student representatives;
- a strong academic core to the curriculum;
- to have more practically based vocational subjects offered alongside the academic;
- more arts subjects on the curriculum;
- improved sports teams and facilities, both mainstream (football, baseball, athletics and basketball) and recreational (rollerblade hockey and skateboarding);
- to have students and parents on the board of management;
- to have improved social and refreshment facilities on site for the whole campus and the community.

The newly elected principal was able to show that the school had taken up the parents' and students' suggestions and that most of their demands had been met or were in the planning stages, with continuing consultation with all concerned. As a result the school was more than holding its own with the new high schools and indeed was over-subscribed for the next academic year. The Principal reported that, 'The enrolment goal of 1,000 students was reached in the first 24 hours and there is now a waiting list.' (Further details of this project can be found in Smith, 1992.)

Vancouver, University of British Columbia

Although I was unable to visit schools in the Vancouver area as they were on a mid-semester break, I was able to establish that there was a similar pattern of school supervision by co-operating teachers supported by teacher fellows or graduate students and a seconded teacher organizer who managed placements. Faculty were involved in school-based work but on the whole the pressure on delivery of lectures and on research output in this very academic university meant that most of the day-to-day work was carried out by graduate students. These graduate students also did the marking and assessment of education students' assignments. Amongst the people I was able to interview was a school district supervisor who told me of the work being done in some school districts which employed many of the key concepts of professional development schools – students working in groups with co-operating teachers, teachers contributing to university-based sessions, and co-operating teachers working with professors on research into teacher preparation.

Penn State, University of Pennsylvania

This university was the closest I saw to the more traditional model of teacher training in the United States in which the practicum was still less important than the university-based course and where most of the teacher trainees I interviewed wanted more school-based work and to be in schools teaching earlier in their courses (they did two years of subject-based studies before commencing two years of teacher preparation). There was a partnership with local schools and there were some faculty staff committed to the idea of more school-based work, but on the whole theoretical courses took precedence. Things were moving, however, and I was able to attend a meeting of the principals of co-operating schools with the schools placement officer and some faculty staff. There was a clear feeling that the education professors were still reluctant to allow students more time in school or earlier visits to schools but there was much agreement about the aims and desired outcomes of the course and the co-operating principals made several useful changes to the curriculum at that meeting.

In one school I was able to see progress towards the PDS ideals. This was an out-of-town elementary school where two young faculty (one professor and one associate professor) spent a lot of time in the school working with the trainees, the teachers and with individual pupils. It was their intention to generate joint research papers from this as well as ensuring the maximum benefit for the students and trainees. The teachers spoke highly of the university supervisors' commitment and enjoyed the opportunity to contribute to the research project.

University of Wisconsin, Madison

This was the university I visited that was most pro-active in creating links between teachers and university professors with even the most senior academics (Ken Zeichner and Carl Grant) involved in school-based projects and committed to the principle of school improvement via the creation of professional development schools with particular reference to the opportunities for education of diverse urban communities. Madison, Wisconsin also had the most widely developed networks of action research with many of its co-operating teachers being ex-graduate students (who had acted as university supervisors) with masters degrees or doctorates and still involved in research from a school base and often still contributing to the university-based courses. At Madison, Wisconsin (rated one of the top research education schools in the United States) I was able to speak to all stakeholders, from the Head of Education, Ken Zeichner, through university supervisors, co-operating teachers and importantly the trainee teachers. Most usefully I was also able to interview the school placement co-ordinator and, in two schools, the master teacher responsible for school-based training – both pre-service and in-service.

One of the interesting aspects of the Madison partnership process was the way in which students were placed in schools. In order to ensure compatibility and good working relationships every student visited three teachers and every teacher was visited by three students and on every visit each completed and submitted a report with a rating. This system was efficiently and sympathetically administered by Jo Richards, an ex-elementary school principal with much experience and under-standing of teaching and teachers. Jo set up the visits, interviewed individual teachers and student teachers and finally sent all of the completed forms to the computer centre for cross-matching. She then monitored the outcomes and the ongoing relationships, arranging changes and new partnerships where existing ones did not work to mutual satisfaction. During the observation it was clear that teachers and trainees appreciated this and that it removed many of the initial problems of working in partnership.

The system employed for the Wisconsin-Madison Elementary Teacher Educa-tion Programme was entitled the Student Teaching Triad and the model showed a partnership between the student teacher, the co-operating teacher and the uni-versity supervisor. Supervisors and co-operating teachers attended university courses (postgraduate credits are necessary for the retention of tenure) in supervision, in their own postgraduate areas and in action research. Of the action research course for co-operating teachers, Ken Zeichner said: 'I feel it's important before they can start having students doing action research they need to experience it themselves and the students need to know that and see them engaging in the same kinds of things.'

Teachers had to pay for these courses and although the education faculty had wanted to deliver them free to co-operating teachers this was not permitted by the university regulations. However, teachers were given other benefits in kind such as parking permits at the university, library membership, priority booking for ball games and for some the status of visiting professor.

It is this university which I will examine in some detail using one of the four schools I visited and studied as a study of the way in which initial teacher preparation was conducted at Madison. In order to focus the research as a case study I will look in detail at the school which most epitomized the espoused principles of the Madison system. This school, which I will call 'Flag Elementary', had many interesting characteristics, including students from a diverse range of backgrounds. It was an orderly school in a well-kept building and had police and security guards patrolling the corridors. Although it was situated in a leafy suburban area of Madison many of its students were bussed in from poorer areas. This was the school which Ken Zeichner had chosen to work in and make his contribution to the school of education's partnership with schools. Ken had particular views on partnership and PDSs and was concerned that 'the dominant model of Professional Development Schools in the US has been a knowledge transmission model ... which many practising teachers have rejected'. The model which he preferred and promulgated was one which employed 'study groups, action research groups, collaborative networks and an emerging grassroots staff development that teachers find very meaningful. It leads to a merging of pre-service and in-service teacher education.' Zeichner went on to explain how the process worked in the school with which he was connected, 'Flag Elementary':

> I work in partnership with the supervisor who is based in school. We work with both the student teachers and the staff in a variety of ways. It leads to a merging of pre-service and in-service teacher education. In a seminar in the school this morning we had both student teachers and teachers learning about the same issues. We bring in teachers to conduct various sessions with the student teachers so the teachers become experts about certain things and it creates a flow of knowledge which goes in both directions. I want to work with teachers in a more equal way. I feel really uncomfortable being seen as the expert disseminating notes to passive teachers. I think I do have things to offer and I'm willing to offer those but within a different kind of relationship and this year Tabachnick and I have been working with the area teachers in building an action research collaborative.

For Zeichner the action research element is the glue which holds together the different aspects of initial teacher training, continuing professional development, professional development schools and the schools/university partnership.

'Flag Elementary' – a case study of a professional development school

In Flag Elementary the post of master teacher was one which was a joint appointment between school and university allowing one person time to both supervise trainee teachers and to be available to help and advise teachers on their in-service needs. (Here at last was the pivotal person in teacher professional development whom I had been searching for since hearing Dorothy Lloyd's lecture about the new teacher training courses at CSU San Marcos.) Ken Zeichner made it clear that having a school-based university supervisor doubling as a master teacher was not a normal arrangement but the result of a grant that the education faculty had squeezed out of the Chancellor's office at the university in order to research the concept.

The university supervisor

As the university supervisor was school-based and also played the role of professional development teacher (sometimes called learning co-ordinator or master teacher) I will examine her role first. (Note that in this school the co-operating teachers are also sometimes called master teachers.) Ms Blanche White (a pseudonym) was a lively and enthusiastic teacher who spoke of the importance of her role:

> The key factors about having an on-site supervisor are consistency and availability. It makes a huge difference to both the master teachers and the student teachers ... when I go into a room to supervise I know [the trainee], I know the master teacher very well, I know her style, I know all the students, I know the community issues. I'm part of life here. In our talks the feedback [the trainees] get is relevant and the suggestions I make are attainable, not just pie in the sky. It's very easy for someone to go in and say what could be better but unless it's based on reality [it isn't much use].

She also spoke of her role in ensuring appropriate placements of trainees with master teachers and the way in which her knowledge ensured mutual benefit from the match:

> It comes from the knowledge that you can put two people together and the kids are going to benefit ... If the kids are benefiting the student teacher is benefiting and, guess what, and so is the master teacher. So it's a pretty good deal.

Blanche also made the important point that the drop-out rate of trainees at her school was lower than average for the course and attributed this to careful placement and close supervision. It wasn't that the relationships were cosy but that in a well-knit community honesty was appreciated:

> When people come to me with questions and criticisms – and sometimes there's truth in them – because we all live together it is easier to work through the truth and come to a positive resolution. Ethically I feel very good because I'm very confident that the people who graduate are going to be excellent teachers and in particular excellent teachers of a diverse population.

The university supervisor would normally run a seminar one day a week in the school and in this case the seminar was co-taught by Blanche and Ken Zeichner. She reported that the seminars were really workshops in which students and master teachers all contributed, choosing topics and working together. The most exciting thing for the trainees, Blanche felt, was the collaborative nature of their training – working together with the teacher and with another trainee:

> They have a unique opportunity to practice supporting each other and they do that. In the seminar they have a peer supervision component. They go through that – observe each other – and they get some pretty exciting things out of that. Another goal I have [for them] is that they are ready to teach pupils from diverse backgrounds – racially, economically and academically ... I like to address these issues head on. There is no time to dance around them – a year is a short time.

In discussing her role as staff development officer Blanche said that she treated student teachers the same as members of staff:

> If I see an article that I think a staff person would enjoy in an area I know they're working in I will give it to them. I do the same thing for the students. It's supervising them plus supporting them the way I would anyone on the staff. We [Blanche and the student teachers] also communicate through journals.

I asked how she overcame the classic dilemma of the mentor of being initially a carer, supporter and confidante and then being the person who had to make the final report on the student teacher, and whether this affected the student teacher's willingness to be honest about their weaknesses. Blanche replied:

> I've never questioned the truth [of what they tell me]. I may not be getting the whole story. But again because I live here stories have a way of unravelling themselves. I can imagine if you were coming in from the Uni and just checking every now and again things could be hidden.

The discussion went on to examine the role of the student teachers' journals in the process of communication. The students felt that they could open up about problems, difficulties and issues in the journal and not have their grade affected. Blanche explained:

> I would never grade a journal – that would go against the whole trust issue. [Instead] the students form a portfolio which they submit – a selection of stuff which they've addressed – lesson plans, reflections on those plans etc. I keep trying to help them identify themes for the portfolio.

Assessment was a process of encouraging trainees to self-assess on each aspect of the course but with Blanche and the head of education (Ken Zeichner) making the final decision on a pass/fail basis. Student teachers were more concerned with what kind of reference their supervisor would give them when they were searching for a job.

Because this was considered to be part of a professional development school project my next question was about the way in which the partnership operated and how teachers benefited from it. Blanche made an interesting analogy here – she felt as culture torn (between the different worlds of the school and university) as many of the children in the school felt coming from their diverse backgrounds to the middle-class academic standards of school.

> This includes issues of time. Where at the university you might say 'Well, maybe some day I might ... '. In the school you need to know now. 'What am I going to do Monday? How am I going to solve this problem now?' You can't 'maybe' in the lives of children. There's also language – a whole set of jargon we don't share. We're both guilty of it but it doesn't mean it's a common language – and there are tensions that come with that.

But there was a powerful and positive move towards partnership that would benefit teachers:

> Right now Ken and I facilitate a self study course here that the staff can take for a university credit and we're working to improve our own practice in a variety of ways together. Ken's part of that is that he's brought in some outside speakers because of the contacts he has which the school wouldn't necessarily have. Teachers set the agenda. But Ken's so well read and the resident expert so he suggests articles to get us started. We are also going to do something on supervision – a mentoring component for people either to qualify or to re-visit their skills. Bringing the university to the school campus is different in itself. It makes it very attractive to a lot of teachers – you don't have to deal with parking. There are some issues that make going to the university unattractive. It is more relevant here – we're talking about us and what we can do to better us.

My final question to Blanche was 'How can you improve the professional development partnership with the university?' Her response was positive and thoughtful:

> I'd like to see more staff from the school involved in methods classes on campus and different personnel from the campus more involved in classes here ... [The problem is time and money.] I tried to get a grant to get a substitute teacher in our building so we could release teachers to go and get on with these things. It was rejected out of hand because one of the reviewers read it and said 'I was in a professional development school once and it didn't work'. I felt they'd made up their minds before they started reading the application. The reality is [if PDSs are going to work] everybody is going to have to do more.

The role of the co-operating teacher (CT)

Co-operating teachers are school-based classsroom teachers who volunteer to take university students on teaching practice. They undergo either a school district or university training and are then responsible for a great deal of the trainee teacher's learning. Ginger Golson, a research student and university supervisor, outlined their role in this way:

> The co-operating teachers are definitely responsible to give feedback [to teacher trainees], introduce them to school and district policies, to provide them with various strategies for creating lessons. [They] introduce them to different ways of working with children with different backgrounds and with different learning needs ... they

give them focused observation, give them written feedback and also verbal feedback. They are required to meet with the university supervisor and the student for a triad conference at least three times in the semester. Co-operating teachers also attend the weekly seminar which I teach in the school. Co-operating teachers ... have a responsibility for all of the prospective teachers that are in their school ... and a responsibility to be a good role model for not only student teachers and children in the classroom but to all educators. We are all in it together to improve the educational system and they must be willing to give the time. It's a role where a person has to be willing to work together with other people knowing that it's nice to have another teacher in the classroom but also that it's a huge responsibility of time and dedication.

One co-operating teacher, 'John Bright', responded lucidly to my questions about his role, and particularly how he was able to influence and maybe change the university's approach to teacher education:

> Maybe we're back to the theory of practice – I have faith that the Uni is talking about different methodologies, certain theoretical backgrounds and I know the kids and I know classrooms so I affect change that way saying, 'These are lovely ideas but how do you put them into practice?' Without the co-operating teacher nothing happens. We tailor some of the student experiences as well. I make a connection with another teacher and send a student over there for an experience or maybe a student teacher needs to shadow our social worker around the neighbourhood for a day to get a different viewpoint. That's totally up to us what we decide, so that's a big influence.

John was an ex Ph.D. student of Ken Zeichner's, an ex-university supervisor, and, like many of the teachers in this district and especially in this school (fifteen of the teachers had taken supervision and action research courses), was still undertaking his own research as part of one of the action research groups of teachers. The same teacher explained why he was part of the teacher education programme and why the professional development school worked well:

> I was on a Ph.D. programme at the university in teacher education ... Because of my interest in teacher education I was a supervisor ... When I moved back into the classroom there was a natural match [as a co-operating teacher]. I didn't want to abandon teaching and Lincoln has a lot of teachers like that. That's why we're a professional development school – we talk about teaching a lot. We are all very much believers in reflection as part of our profession. The student teachers are involved in self-study. The school culture is one of reflection and study and that seems to be an important thing for student teachers to understand. You don't just learn a programme and implement it and coast to retirement. You're always working and you're always learning.

The Madison model required the teacher to stay in the classroom with student teachers and asked for a high degree of co-operative teaching. John Bright explained how he went about mentoring student teachers and what was in it for himself and his school students.

> The student I now have has been talking a lot about the gap between theory and practice. Now we're trying to build the bridge into practice with good management using all sorts of skills. Without the management you never get the chance to practice those lovely theories ... I like the 'Why?' question. I encourage student teachers to ask me why I do stuff and I tell them to hit me with a stick if I say 'I've always done it

that way.' ... I like to catch myself and say ... 'Why have I always done it this way?' I also like beginning teachers coming in with their fresh vision and their new knowledge and I like to collaborate with them. I've been led into directions with student teachers that I've never dreamed myself so it keeps me aware of what's happening. It's nice to have another adult learner in the room. We get more done so it's better for the kids – the kids learn to make an adjustment to several adults not just me. So it's a win win situation. What's in it for the school is I hope a culture of learning – we are all involved in learning and helping each other to learn.

John Bright's student, 'Rose', reported that she was at an advantage training in a professional development school:

When I compare myself to my room mate [who is training in another school] I feel I get a more immediate chance to try things out and experiment and go back to classes at Uni with real life experiences. I think here in this school each teacher has completely different styles and skills – watching them is amazing. I pick up different tricks and skills from each person. I told one teacher, 'I don't want you to tell me I'm doing everything alright' or 'Oh! you're doing fine'. I want you to say, 'Maybe this is something you can work on.' It seems to me that they felt really comfortable giving constructive criticism. The feedback I've got has been pretty good and there is informal feedback every day and some more formal written feedback and also peer supervisions.

Rose also referred to the role of other student teachers in providing peer supervision and explained why it was helpful and unthreatening:

It's a clinical supervision with four loosely structured questions but sometimes we ask, 'Is there something specific you want me to look for?' Getting criticism from someone who is struggling with the same things at the same time is really easy to accept. When they say, 'I notice you were struggling with this', I won't take it as a value test so much because he was struggling with it yesterday or he's struggling with it now. So it's kind of, 'We're in this together' and we're experiencing the same things. It's like watching yourself teach – a window to yourself.

Summary

This case study school represented the ideal for Ken Zeichner's project. He had set up a study base there for students and teachers to learn together under the supervision of university tutors, the school master teacher and himself. It was a most interesting example of a theoretical and research-based approach to professional development schools as a means of improving teacher training and linking it to programmes for continuing professional development and education for diversity. It was working well, in the view of all those I interviewed and was creating a buzz of excitement amongst them because they felt they were privileged to be part of the project.

It was clear that although the Madison project was an excellent example of good school/university partnership in school improvement with a range of good relationships producing good results and one outstanding professional development school, the faculty as a whole was locked into a more traditional model which Zeichner and some of his colleagues were attempting to break down. The problems that they faced were the universal ones of time and money. Education faculty members were normally expected to spend their time doing research and delivering courses, and teachers were not usually given sufficient time and responsibility to become fully involved in teacher education. This project, which empowered all the stakeholders in the process of teacher education at both initial and in-service levels, was well funded and well supported by senior academics and school administrators – so it worked. As the master teacher indicated, not all academics or administrators were convinced the professional development schools would work well enough to gain the extra funding they needed.

Because of his interest in PDSs and his international reputation for research and writing about teacher training, Ken Zeichner was one of the National Committee for the Accreditation of Teacher Education group who were looking at the impact of PDSs on partnerships in teacher training and developing national standards for these partnerships.

The other interesting international connection which Zeichner made with his Madison set up of networking, study groups and teacher action research networks was with the Committee for Action Research Networks. Convinced that teacher knowledge and teacher research was as valuable as mainstream academic research Zeichner provided local, national and international opportunities for teacher-generated knowledge to be promulgated and published. The Madison Action Research Network publishes and circulates papers from many groups, has regular meetings and conferences (including a locally networked television programme for teacher researchers) and has built professional academic pride amongst participating teachers. The international connection was reinforced when Zeichner introduced a young English doctoral student to act as discussant in his place on one of the papers delivered at the New York meeting of the American Educational Research Association.

Conclusion

The following are ways in which key participants in school/university partnerships and professional development schools can help to improve schools and thus improve children's learning.

1. School students

School students deserve the best teaching they can get. Where professional development schools identify good teachers to become master teachers/co-operating teachers the possibility exists for those teachers to pass on their skills in team-teaching situations where the students continue to get good teaching with the added advantage of having an extra intelligent adult helping them, listening to them, and giving them up-to-date information. The co-operating teacher is on their mettle whilst demonstrating and modelling planning, preparation and teaching techniques, thus the students benefit from good lessons. There is also a growth of awareness in the co-operating teacher as they model reflection and seek to explain and justify their methods. Good trainee teachers bring with them to schools new ideas, up-to-date knowledge of their subjects and recent research-based methodological improvements. If they are skilfully inducted into teaching, with continued master teacher presence until their management is secure, the students should benefit from their enthusiasm and new approaches. It is a key aspect of the professional development schools that team teaching goes on for much of the trainees' time in the school in order that students are not abandoned to unskilled trainees. The co-operating teacher has a key role in judging when and for how long the trainee can be left to find their feet with a class whilst maintaining responsibility for maximizing the students' learning.

2. Trainee teachers

Trainee teachers have been shown by researchers in both the US and the UK to be best able to perform when they are placed in schools with good practice and with teacher supervisors with whom they are able to relate. The waste of talent and money involved in placing trainee teachers in very difficult schools where they are 'thrown in the deep end to sink or swim' or where they are left to get on with it because 'the university should have prepared them' is enormous. In schools where they are committed to giving their students the best possible education they are also concerned to train the next generation of teachers to be secure, competent contributors to student learning. Treating trainees as a source of free time for hard-pressed teachers or as exemplars for poor teachers may be useful in the short term but too often leads to trainees merely surviving or at worst leaving the course. Professional development schools often appoint a professional tutor to ensure that trainee teachers are well supported by their supervising teachers and that the school has a role in inducting and training them. Where university tutors work in the schools, either alongside the teacher and trainee or presenting and chairing seminars there is a breaking down of the oft-proclaimed theory/practice divide. Most university teaching practice supervisors are ex-teachers who have extended their studies and have much to offer the training triad. Working together makes the discussion of problems an open and shared one and learning together reinforces the idea of all being involved in continuing professional development. Where students are able to witness teachers and professors reflecting and discussing issues they are gaining experience and having processes modelled for them. The in-service learning process is seen to be an aspect of a working teacher's life, and the trainee, sometimes able to contribute specialist knowledge and recent learning to the teachers, can not only be part of that but recognize that continuing professional development will be part of their future professional life. When, as at Madison, the triad are jointly involved in reflection through action research projects which are shared at workshops and conferences and promulgated via university supported publications, it becomes even clearer that all involved can be learners and all involved can contribute to the creation of new professional knowledge.

3. Master teachers/professional development co-ordinators

This is, or can be, the pivotal role in the whole-school improvement process. Increasingly put off by the demands of administration in senior posts in schools, many ambitious teachers see a future for themselves in acting as mentor, supervisor and trainer in their schools. Many of these people, often well qualified and looking for new challenges, have begun by acting as supervisors for teaching students or newly qualified teachers and seen that there are links with other needs in the school including appraisal and continuing professional development. They are often well connected with university faculties and make contributions both in their schools and in the universities to teacher training programmes and sometimes to in-service programmes. These connections make them able to advise colleagues on which in-service courses are available and how they can enrol on them. In some cases they set up school-based programmes of in-service training tailored to the school's development plan and meeting the teachers' needs identified in the appraisal programmes. They have contacts to enable them to invite university personnel to contribute to courses and conferences and are able to suggest topics for research papers for colleagues and help them find ways of publishing them through action research networks and through connections with universities. It is often they who make applications for grants to extend the school's continuing professional development culture and they who lead their schools in seeking awards for achievement such as the Investing in People kitemark, City Technology College status and Centre of Excellence awards.

4. University supervisors (university adjuncts)

There are distinct differences here between the United States and England. In America many of these posts are held by teachers undertaking research degrees at universities and they naturally have recent and relevant experience of working in schools which enables them to relate to teachers, trainees and students on a practical level. At the same time many of them are also studying aspects of teaching at a theoretical level and researching in schools, so they are aware of current theoretical perspectives on their subjects and on pedagogical topics. They are often also well connected with university faculty and sometimes part of research teams with senior faculty looking at key topics in current educational debates (such as school improvement and education for diversity), and as such can be helpful to both trainees and teachers in their studies and continuing professional development. The most exciting work I came across in the US was where faculty professors with a keen interest in school improvement worked together with supervisors, teachers and students on particular topics – teaching and learning together and ensuring student development.

In England, supervision is largely carried out by university staff, though there are increasingly examples of teacher fellows and retired teachers taking on supervision. School-based teacher training is the norm now in England with either shared supervision, in which university and teacher supervisors make alternate observations, or school-based supervision, in which the school undertakes all of the supervision with occasional visits from the university to ensure the programme is working. Although this has led to a growth in confidence, skill and qualification amongst the school supervisors/teacher mentors, there have been few examples of universities becoming as closely involved in school improvement programmes as I observed in the US. There are some examples of ways in which university supervisors have worked with graduate students, undertaking advanced studies, to examine ways in which mentoring can be developed to encompass wider school improvement issues, such as the induction and training of newly qualified teachers and the role of staff development officer, ensuring that appraisal outcomes are linked to school development plans and that staff undertake continuing professional development to attain the resulting targets. Generally, however, the university supervisor is concerned with quality assurance and with maintaining links with schools as the government seeks to drive schools and universities apart with its programme for school-centred teacher education in which schools undertake the whole of teacher training and connections with universities are unnecessary.

5. University lecturers/professors

Experts in their subjects or in pedagogy, university professors are concerned to create and maintain proper academic rigour in teacher education and training and to combat the reductionism of governments concerned to achieve short-term recruitment targets cheaply and quickly. It is the role of professors in education not only to teach trainee teachers but to create programmes of postgraduate work that meet the continuing professional development needs of teachers. They are also concerned to publish research into new ideas and methodologies, keeping their universities at the forefront of education thinking and investigating key issues of their times. At their very best these professors are able to balance the demands of academic life with the rigours of working in schools, with teachers, trainees and with the students, in order that what they are publishing is recognizable and relevant to practitioners. Obviously some of their work will be at the cutting-edge of theory and will be intended to be read and discussed by academic peers, but unless they are able to demonstrate that they understand the everyday world in which their students, graduates and postgraduates have to work, their credibility will soon fade. At their best these lecturers and professors are able to work in partnership with all involved in school improvement and educational development, contributing their skill and knowledge in the world of research and publication and enabling teachers and trainees to reflect their worlds. In many cases joint publications showing views of university faculty, teachers and trainees are not only fascinating insights from different viewpoints but together move towards new syntheses of understanding of educational issues.

6. Head teachers (school principals) and local educational area administrators (school district supervisors)

These important gatekeepers of time and money are considered together because of the complexity of the various methods of organizing and managing schools in each country and between the two countries. For school improvement to succeed, either via school/university partnerships or through the professional development schools' movement, there needs to be the political and administrative will and there needs to be investment. We have seen already that these developments are often brought about by the enthusiasm of the few and that there are all too often obstacles in the way of school improvement from traditionalism and conservatism. Administrations which recognize the need for school improvement would do well to look to universities and to their own employees with advanced qualifications for initial advice. The best practice seems to be to employ a master teacher or professional development co-ordinator who can pull together the advantages of university, district and school-based inputs into initial training, induction of new staff and continuing professional development. Appraisal and inspection can produce assessment of achievement and targets for development but there will need to be clearly targeted development led by enthusiasts if improvement in student learning and school results are to be achieved. Where no investment is made and teachers are expected to undertake initial teacher training, help mentor new teachers and undertake their own development without release or reward, there is often a reaction and quality falls off as cynicism sets in. On the other hand, where teachers are led as a team towards enhanced status and improved conditions and results in the school, they will often put in a great deal of unpaid time to be part of a success. The administration which manages to balance reasonable support, encouragement, reward and recognition with clear assessment, target-setting and investment is the one which is most likely to succeed.

Chapter 10

Conclusion

In our concluding remarks, we wish to place our review of the structures and processes of initial training and continuing professional development into some kind of broader context. The nature of teacher education symbolizes the prevailing attitudes towards teaching and learning in general – and the kind of society which is desirable now and in the future. In this respect, we are possibly in uncharted waters since there appears to be a consensus between the major British political parties. There is an apparent uncontested assumption of a functional relationship between schooling and social and economic goals; that if education is radically improved the result will be a more competitive, cohesive society. In the quest to place the blame for alleged moral, social and economic decline, teachers have received more than their fair share and, in turn, those responsible for their initial and continuing professional education are viewed as the main culprits since they have had the means, in an indirect manner, to influence generations of children.

It is not really plausible to ascribe this kind of power to teacher educators, but it has been proved to be convenient if there is a will to alter, in a fundamental manner, the nature of the system, although if the political rhetoric is stripped out it is possible to arrive at a calmer view of the current practice. As far as initial training is concerned, four approaches can be identified (Archer and Hogbin, 1995, p. 8):

- the *academic* approach – where emphasis is placed upon liberal education, with an implicit criticism of much teacher education for its lack of intellectual rigour;
- the *apprenticeship* approach – where the emphasis is on teaching as a craft and where teaching is understood as training;
- the *experiential* approach – where the emphasis is on the self-perceived needs and concerns of prospective teachers, and where teacher education involves individual shifts of perception about themselves as teachers;

- the *managerial* approach – where the emphasis is on the organization of teacher education and how the specific observable skills of teaching are related to pupil learning.

These approaches should be viewed as ideal types since reality suggests a good deal of overlap. Nonetheless, they may help to clarify the tensions which beset the system. The *academic* approach derives from the western university tradition, yet there is a strong argument that this is inappropriate for the preparation of teachers where the demand is for practical application, against the backcloth of articulated social demands. If an educated population is seen in the same way as a healthy population, that is, that they are indicators of a 'good' society, then the measure of both of these is a matter for political judgement. When a decision is made to become a teacher and to enter a programme of professional preparation it is often on the basis of a commitment to a set of socially constructed, if not politically constructed, expectations. The *academic* approach, on this basis, may simply be too much of an indulgence; that while it is perfectly legitimate for a liberal arts programme, it has little relevance for a course of what is essentially vocational training. There is little chance that there will be a return to the domination of this kind of model for either initial training or continuing professional development; it is politically risky in an era of 'accountability' and 'value for money' – and, particularly, where education is now seen as the panacea for a variety of social and economic ills.

On the other hand, the total elimination of the *academic* approach may significantly change the image of initial teacher education programmes, especially at undergraduate level, in the eyes of prospective students. In an era when increasing numbers of young people are entering higher education, and when final decisions on occupational destination are further postponed, there is the possibility that an entirely non-academic approach to teacher education will endow it with a quite different status, characteristic of the nineteenth and early twentieth centuries, where it was regarded more as craft training or as an extended form of secondary schooling.

So, in view of a possible revitalization of the British *apprenticeship* 'system', it might be envisaged that initial teacher education should revert to this model which, after all, has underpinned much of the process of acculturation which occurs in the workplace. Traditionally, there are important elements of apprenticeship in the induction process for new entrants to the profession, where the experienced 'master/mistress' acts in a hierarchically defined manner towards the novice. Yet, the structure of employment in schools has changed, as such structures everywhere have changed, and this has meant that it can no longer be assumed that an age-related hierarchy will prevail. Older, more experienced, teachers are now considered a drag on the market and a drain on resources as schools seek to balance their budgets and maintain their competitive edge. As a corollary, an increasing number, including a good many head teachers and others in senior positions, have sought and gained early retirement, thus altering the age profile of the staff in a radical manner. Newly qualified teachers may find that in English schools in the dying days of the twentieth century there will be relatively few 'master craftsmen/women' of long years' standing to guide them in their first years of teaching. Likewise, in an era of partnership, the school-based learning context for initial training students takes on a different look as placements are secured with teachers barely beyond newly qualified teacher stage.

In any case, there must be grave doubts as to whether the *apprenticeship* approach is able to ensure an authentic sharing of expertise. In the past, it frequently meant little more than a period of time-serving, and, as Hake has pointed out, 'real partnership is not defined in terms of the ratio of time spent in one place or the other. Nor can it be divided into neat blocks of ideas or tasks delivered by the school or the university' (Hake, 1993, p. 33). The result might very well be a system where the two 'deliverers' operate quite separately, where the university-based programme merely offers some kind of INSET for apprentice teachers.

What of the *experiential* model? Notionally, there remains an expectation that teachers and students in preparation are required to be reflective and self-evaluative; in short, to learn from experience. In recent years we have encountered a veritable panoply of published works, conferences and workshops which expound the virtues of 'the reflective practitioner'. The notion has, of course, provided a means of bridging the transition between initial training and continuing professional development where action research is revealed as a means both of improving practice and (allegedly) of contributing to the store of educational knowledge. In the current climate, the *experiential* approach may yet retain a legitimate role in the preparation of teachers; much will depend on the boundaries which are placed around the realm of 'self-perceived needs and concerns' which characterize this model. If such needs and concerns are strictly defined in terms of the ability to deliver the National Curriculum in an effective manner, or of the capacity to ensure a high grade following an OFSTED inspection, then it might be hoped that a reflective approach to teaching might make an effective contribution to improved practice. (A particularly effective use of reflective practice as action research is discussed in Chapter 9 of this volume.)

We doubt, however, that there will be much to challenge, in the foreseeable future, the *managerial* approach to teacher education. This does suggest a less than optimistic view since managerialism has frequently been seen as a contributory factor to, if not the cause of, a rather cynical perspective on the initial training process. It is clear that there will continue to be an emphasis upon the manner in which teacher education is actually organized and, given the importance of measured *competence* as the criterion for the granting of qualified teacher status, the focus will increasingly be on observable teacher behaviours. Competence is part of the public realm, as opposed to understanding and appreciation which are essentially private matters and therefore of little significance to agencies charged with issues of quality control and accreditation in the field of teacher education. If the school system is not producing sufficiently qualified young people to make an effective contribution to the fortunes of the nation-state then fine-tuning (or not-so-fine tuning) of the process of teacher education should be undertaken to ensure that lack of competence on the part of students undergoing initial training is remedied.

At the end of the day, some might wonder what all the fuss has been about. There is the familiar argument that no matter whether there are refinements of partnership arrangements, a readiness to respond to OFSTED in a reasoned manner, or a National Curriculum which ensures, for those on primary programmes, competence to teach children to read, things might just continue in the same old way. Perhaps, though, this is more in hope than in anticipation, reflecting the desire of some university tutors to retain their functions vis-à-vis trainee teachers, based upon the now unfashionable and derided formulae of the 1960s and 1970s, and to keep the role of schools firmly under their control. It is probable, however, that few of the participants in initial teacher education programmes would wish to adhere to a static approach and that, in reality, there is a great deal more give and take on all sides. The ritual dance which has conventionally accompanied the process of preparation for the classroom has never been viewed as wholly satisfactory by students, tutors or schools and there is little evidence to suggest that closer collaboration between schools and universities has ever been seriously challenged. Moreover, there is more than the faintest suspicion that many of those university academics involved in teacher education who dealt in rarified theory might have felt more at home in social science faculties had they had the opportunity to join them. On the other side, schools are conscious of their limitations and there is probably a recognition that initial training requires a judicious combination of theory and practice which is not solely located within either schools or universities.

Perhaps the way forward is summed up neatly by Archer and Hogbin (1995, p. 46) who suggest that teachers and tutors should form collaborative partnerships which are a combination of:

a. the breadth of experience, access to research, and concentration of resources and scarce expertise to be found in higher education, plus
b. the professional experience of many teachers.

This goes for the entire process of teacher education which should be viewed as a continuum, from initial training, through induction, to continuing professional development via INSET. While this is scarcely radical and is little more than is being commonly uttered by those with a commonsense approach to the matter, it possibly needs to be emphasized, since a real collaboration, devoid of suspicion and demarcation anxieties, may just transcend the whims of political masters. Education in general and teacher education in particular will continue to be highly politicized at the level of policy-making and it is perfectly legitimate that it should be that way since the fundamental concern is with societal goals. It would be difficult to guard against those charged with the implementation of policy at the 'chalk-face' finding space in which to subvert such stated goals; perhaps, though, that is a price worth paying if the aim is to produce knowledgeable, reflective, imaginative and – yes – competent teachers.

Postscript

Teacher education in England and Wales seemed like a never-ending story so that just after the concluding chapter had been written another one appeared from a different contributor: the Dearing Report on Higher Education (1997). While the DfEE, TTA and OFSTED had proceeded in a more or less uniform direction – with an emphasis upon competences, outcomes and measurement, and latterly, standards (DfEE 10/97) – those who adopted a critical stance towards this new paradigm were increasingly voices in the wilderness. It remained to be seen whether Dearing was to have legitimacy and whether, more importantly, the report was to have any impact upon the future course of teacher education.

In acknowledging the significantly increased role played by schools, questions were raised about the contribution of higher education institutions (HEIs) to initial teacher education. It was fairly clear that Dearing had a good deal of anxiety about the apparent threats to the role of HEIs and challenged the view that HE provision was inadequate in this respect, and concluded that 'higher education does provide a satisfactory context for the training and education of teachers' (para. 62). The perception of inadequacy, it was suggested, is the possible outcome of 'a perceived hostility towards higher education and a lack of understanding about its role in TET [teacher education and training]' (para. 60).

Yet, Dearing was by no means hostile to the notion of partnership in TET; on the contrary, he believed that it provided the way forward as long as the roles of each partner were carefully outlined, demonstrating their complementarity. Thus:

> Higher education should provide an environment in which it is possible for trainees to study core academic subjects to a high standard and to develop knowledge and understanding about different methods of teaching and the ways in which children learn. It should provide the context in which trainees develop an ability to think critically about, and reflect on, teaching practice and provide breadth of perspective, as well as exposure to other disciplines and access to pedagogic research. HE should also have a role in training teaching mentors and in providing CPD that builds upon ITT. (para. 62)

It is difficult to detect a difference between this view of the role of HE in teacher education and those views which prevailed until the changes brought about with advent of CATE. It seems fairly clear that Dearing expressed some sensitivity to those who had perceived a growing hostility to the role of higher education in the preparation of teachers and, accordingly, set out his own stall in respect of the legitimate role of HEIs. Unashamedly, he stated: 'Successful teachers should ... have an adequate knowledge of educational theory on which to develop their classroom skills' (para. 63), but, at the same time, also believed that HEIs could perform this role successfully within school-based teacher training schemes such as SCITT. On the other hand, Dearing considered that CPD would be the more significant arena for HEIs and the provision of theoretical understanding in TET since there would not be the encumbrance of having to instil the basic skills and competencies of pedagogy.

At a more practical level, Dearing was unequivocal in stating that the success of partnership depended on stability and adequate financial arrangements, neither of which appeared to be in place (para. 66), and that the whole enterprise had not been properly costed. The more general resource implications for schools – time as well as money – had made themselves apparent, particularly in respect of the competing pressures of demand for partnership arrangements on the part of schools and the perceived demands of OFSTED. Anecdotally, one of the authors who had previously been involved in the placement of students in schools had noted the reluctance and sometimes polite refusal of some head teachers to have ITT students in their schools at all, let alone on a partnership basis. At the same time, while there remained a strongly held view that the education and care of children should take precedence over other objectives as far as schools are concerned, Dearing concluded that there must be a clearer expectation that all schools should be involved in TET both in terms of ITT and CPD. It required a much more formal basis for partnership arrangements as well as a tighter and more comprehensive system of quality assurance and control (para. 68). The context for this should be a system of networks of schools, HEIs and LEAs which would form regional centres for the delivery of TET of all kinds (para. 69).

Recently, it was possible to detect some piecemeal change in the direction proposed by Dearing, but it seemed ad hoc and reflected local initiative rather than the implementation of a coherent national policy. However, the Dearing Report soon appeared to be side-lined by central government as it was eclipsed by the seemingly ever-increasing power of the DfEE. Accordingly, criteria were published which all initial teacher training programmes were required to meet, and specified ITT national curricula in English, mathematics, science and the use of information and communications technology (DfEE, 1998). Leaving aside central government edicts, the focus must remain on the importance of will combined with a readiness to make the appropriate resources available. It is these which are required to ensure that partnership arrangements are more than paying lip-service to some vaguely defined notion. Unless that happens, partnership might well remain a mechanism which results in all parties being less than satisfied, not least those at the sharp end of the process, the students who will become the next generation of classroom teachers.

Bibliography

Abell, S. K., Dillon, D. R., Hopkins, C. J., McInery, W. D. and O'Brien, D. G. (1995) '"Somebody to count on": Mentor/intern relationships in a beginning teacher internship program.' *Teaching and Teacher Education*, **11**(2), 173–88.

Acton, R., Kirkham, G. and Smith, P. (1992) *Mentoring: A Core Skills Pack*. Crewe and Alsager College.

Alexander, R., Rose, J. and Woodhead, C. (1992) *Curriculum Organization and Classroom Practice in Primary Schools: A Discussion Paper* (Department of Education and Science). London: HMSO.

Allen, J., Maude, P., Street-Porter, R. and Turner, M. (1994) 'Report on the evaluation of the Essex partnership induction scheme.' EDAS unpublished.

Andrews, I. H. (1986) 'Five Paradigms of Induction programmes in Teacher Education.' University of Bradford Ph.D. thesis.

Andrews, I. H. (1987) 'Induction programmes: staff development opportunities for beginning experience of teachers.' In Wideen and Andrews (1987).

Archer, M. and Hogbin, J. (1995) *The Place of Autonomy in Primary Initial Teacher Training*. Manchester: Didsbury School of Education, Manchester Metropolitan University.

Argyris, C. (1965) *Organization and Innovation*. New York: Richard D. Irwin.

Baker, K. (1977) 'Helping probationers as staff development.' *Journal of Applied Educational Studies*, **6**(2).

Barber, M. (1995) 'Reconstructing the teaching profession.' *Journal of Education for Teaching*, **21**(1), 75–85.

Bash, L. and Best, R. (1992) 'An evaluation of schools-based supervision of teaching practice with respect to a pilot exercise involving a small group of first year BEd students.' Unpublished.

Becker, H. S., Geer, B. and Hughes, E. (1961) *Boys in White*. Chicago: Chicago University Press.

Behrstock, S. (ed.) (1973) *Continuity in Teacher Education*. Report of WCOTP Conference, Morges, Switzerland.

Benner, P. (1982) 'From novice to expert.' *American Journal of Nursing*, **82**(3).

Berrill, M. (1991) 'Notes on Challney School induction and profiling.' Unpublished.

Besançon, K., Arts, J., Bash, L., Adermann, G., Kocsis, M., Pusztay, J., Schouten, T. and Zadori, L. (1996) *Survey of the Teacher Training System and Recommendation for Evolution: A Report on the Situation in Hungary*. Eindhoven: Pedagogisch Technische Hogeschool, The Netherlands.

Bines, H. and Welton, J. (1995) *Managing Partnership in Teacher Training and Development*. London: Routledge.

Blair, S. and Bercik, J. T. (1987) 'Teacher induction: a survey of experienced teachers.' ERIC DOC ED 303405.

Blake, D., Hanley, V., Jennings, M. and Lloyd, M. (1995) *Researching School-based Teacher Education*. Aldershot: Avebury.

Blake, D., Rose, J. and Woodhead, C. (1996) 'Change in teacher education: interpreting and experiencing new professional roles.' *European Journal of Teacher Education*, **19**(1), 19–34.

Bolam, R. (1973a) *Induction Programmes for Probationary Teachers*. Bristol: University of Bristol.

Bolam, R. (1973b) 'Continuity in teacher education.' In Behrstock (1973).

Bolam, R. (1975a) *Teacher Induction Pilot Scheme, National Evaluation Project: Final Report*. Bristol: University of Bristol School of Education.

Bolam, R. (1975b) 'The supervisory role of the teacher tutor: a complex innovation.' *Research Intelligence*, **1**(2).

Bolam, R. (1976) 'Resources for INSET.' *British Journal of In-Service Education*, **2**(3).

Bolam, R. (1977) 'Training the teachers.' *Trends in Education*, **3**.

Bolam, R. (1984) 'Induction of beginning teachers.' In Husen and Postlewaite (1984).

Bolam, R., Baker, K. and McMahon, A. (1979) *The Teacher Induction Pilot Schemes (TIPS) Project: National Evaluation Report*. Bristol: University of Bristol School of Education.

Boles, K. (1994) 'Teacher leadership in a professional development school.' Paper presented at American Educational Research Association Meeting, New Orleans.

Booth, M. (1993) 'The effectiveness and role of the mentor in school: the students' view.' *Cambridge Journal of Education*, **23**(2).

Booth, M., Furlong, J. and Wilkin, M. (eds) (1990) *Partnership in Initial Teacher Training*. London: Cassell.

Bouchard, T. and Hull, B. (1970) 'A pilot study of problems and practices in the induction of beginning teachers.' ERIC DOC ED 040157.

Brainard, F. (1989) *Professional Development Schools: Status as of 1989*. Seattle: Institute for the Study of Educational Policy, University of Washington.

Broadfoot, P. (1994) 'Profiling as an educative process.' Paper delivered at Anglia Polytechnic University Conference on Profiling and the Professional Development of Teachers.

Bullough, R. V., Kauchak, D., Crow, N. A., Hobbs, S. and Stokes, D. (1996) 'Professional development schools: catalysts for teacher and school change.' Paper presented at American Educational Research Association Meeting, New York.

Burke, P. and Schmidt, W. (1984) 'Entry assistance: a promising practice.' *Action in Teacher Education*, **6**(1–2).

Bush, R. (1966) *The Real World of the Beginning Teacher*. Washington, DC: National Education Association.

Calderhead, J. (1994) 'Profiling: from philosophy to practice.' Paper presented to Conference on Profiling, Anglia Polytechnic University, November 1994.

Cameron-Jones, M. (1991) *Training Teachers: A Practical Guide*. Edinburgh: Scottish Council for Research in Education.

Cameron-Jones, M. and O'Hara, P. (1994) 'What employers want to read about new teachers.' *Journal of Education for Teaching*, **20**(4), 203–14.

Campbell, J. (1994) *Teacher's Workload*. London: Association of Teachers and Lecturers.

Carnegie Forum on Education and Economy (1986) *A Nation Prepared: Teachers for the 21st Century*. New York: Carnegie Forum on Education and Economy.

Carr, D. (1993) 'Questions of competence.' *British Journal of Educational Studies*, **41**(3), 253–71.

Central Advisory Council for England (1967) *Children and Their Primary Schools* (The Plowden Report). London: HMSO.

Clutterbuck, D. (1991) *Everyone Needs a Mentor*. London: Institute of Personnel Management.

Cobban, I. (1976) 'A training model for the teacher tutor role.' *British Journal of In-Service Education*, **2**(3).

Cogan, M. (1973) *Clinical Supervision*. New York: Houghton Mifflin.

Cole, A. L. (1990) 'Helping teachers become "real": opportunities in teacher induction.' *Journal of Staff Development*, **11**(4).

Conner, K., Conner, S. and Jennings, M. (1975) 'The new teacher's problems.' *London Educational Review*, Spring, **4**(1).

Cook, S. A. and McClean, B. (1995) 'The professional development school in Canada: one partnership experience.' *McGill Journal of Education*, Fall, **30**, 311–21.

Cowen, R. (1990) 'Teacher education: a comparative view.' In Graves (1990).

Crawley, F. (1990) 'ILEA and induction of new staff: a co-ordinator's view.' *Primary Teaching Studies*, **5**(2).

Daloz, L. (1986) *Effective Teaching and Mentoring: Realizing the Transformational Power of Adult Learning*. San Francisco: Jossey-Bass.

Darling-Hammond, L. (1994) *Professional Development Schools: Schools for Developing a Profession*. London and New York: Teachers College Press.

Davies, I. (1993) 'Using profiling in initial teacher education: key issues arising from experience.' *Journal of Further and Higher Education*, **17**(2).

Davis, J. (1980) 'Training the teacher tutors.' In Bolam et al. (1979).

Dawkins, J. (1979) 'Progress on INSET.' *Education*, 11 May.

Dearing, R. (1997) *Report of the National Committee of Inquiry into Higher Education*. London: HMSO.

Department of Education and Science (1972a) *The Education and Training of Teachers* (The James Report). London: HMSO.

Department of Education and Science (1972b) *Education: A Framework for Expansion*. London: HMSO.

Department of Education and Science (1976) *Helping New Teachers*. London: HMSO.

Department of Education and Science (1982) *The New Teacher in School*. London: HMSO.

Department of Education and Science (1983a) *Assistance for Probationers from School and LEA Staff*, Administrative Memorandum 1/83. London: HMSO.

Department of Education and Science (1983b) *Teaching Quality*. London: HMSO.

Department of Education and Science (1988a) *The New Teacher in School*. London: HMSO.

Department of Education and Science (1988b) *The Education Reform Act*. London: HMSO.

Department of Education and Science (1992a) *Induction of Newly Qualified Teachers*, Administrative Memorandum 2/92. London: HMSO.

Department of Education and Science (1992b) *The Induction and Probation of New Teachers 1988–1991*, Administrative Memorandum 62/92. London: HMSO.

Department for Education (1992) *Initial Teacher Training (Secondary Phase) Circular No. 9/92*. London: DFE.

Department for Education (1993) *The Initial Training of Primary School Teachers: New Criteria for Courses*, Circular 14/93. London: HMSO.

Department for Education and Employment (1997) *Circular 10/97*. London: HMSO.

Department for Education and Employment (1998) *Circular 4/98*. London: HMSO.

Dreyfus, H. L. and Dreyfus, S. E. (1984) 'Putting computers in their place: analysis versus intuition in the classroom.' In Sloan, D. (ed.) *The Computer in Education: A Critical Perspective*. Columbia, NY: Teachers College Press.

Driscoll, A. et al. (1985) 'Designing a mentor system for beginning teachers.' *Journal of Staff Development*, October.

Earley, P. (1992) *Beyond Initial Teacher Training: Induction and the Role of the LEA.* Slough: National Foundation for Educational Research.

Earley, P. (1994) *Improvement through Inspection? Complementary Approaches to School Development.* London: David Fulton.

Earley, P. (1997) 'External inspectors, "failing schools" and the role of governing bodies.' *School Leadership and Management,* **17**(3).

Earley, P. and Kinder, K. (1994) *Initiation Rights: Effective Induction Practices for New Teachers.* Slough: National Foundation for Educational Research.

Edwards, A. and Collison, J. (1996) *Mentoring and Developing Practice in Schools: Supporting Student Teacher Learning in Schools.* Buckingham and Philadelphia: Open University Press.

Eraut, M. (1985) 'Knowledge creation and knowledge use in professional contexts.' *Studies in Higher Education,* **10**(2).

Eraut, M. (1989) 'Initial teacher training and the NVQ model.' In Burke, J. W. *Competency Based Education and Training.* Lewes: Falmer Press.

Etheridge, C. P. (1989) 'Acquiring the teaching culture: how beginners embrace practices different from university teachings.' *Qualitative Studies in Education,* **2**(4).

Evans, I., Abbott, I., Goodyear, R., Pritchard, A. (1996) 'Developing the mentoring role: some research conclusions.' *Mentoring and Tutoring,* **4**(1).

Evans, N. (1978) *Beginning Teaching in Professional Partnership.* London: Hodder & Stoughton.

Fenwick, A., Assister, A. and Nixon, N. (1992) *Profiling in Higher Education.* London: Council for National Academic Awards in conjunction with Employment Department.

Fenwick, A. and Nixon, N. (1992) *Profiling and Assessment of Work-based Learning: An Annotated Bibliography.* London: Council for National Academic Awards.

Fidler, B. (1996) *Strategic Planning for School Improvement.* Education Management and Administration Society.

Field, B. and Field, T. (eds) (1994) *Teachers as Mentors: A Practical Guide.* London: Falmer Press.

Fish, D. (1989) *Learning Through Practice in Initial Teacher Education.* London: Kogan Page.

Fish, D. (1995) *Quality Mentoring for Students: A Principled Approach to Practice.* London: David Fulton.

Fox, S. M. and Singletary, T. (1986) 'Deductions about supportive induction.' *Journal of Teacher Education,* **37**(1).

Freshour, D. J. and Holman, R. W. (1990) 'Orienting new teachers for maximum effectiveness.' *NASSP Bulletin,* **74**(527), 78–83.

Fullan, M. (1991) *The New Meaning of Educational Change.* London: Cassell.

Fullan, M. (1992) *Successful School Improvement: The Implementation Perspective.* Buckingham: Open University Press.

Fullan, M. and Connelly, M. (1987) *Teacher Education.* Chicago: University of Chicago Press.

Furlong, J. (1994) 'The limits of competence: a cautionary note on Circular 9/92.' Paper delivered at British Educational Research Association Conference, Oxford.

Furlong, J., Maynard, M., Miles, S. and Wilkin, M. (1994) *Secondary Active Mentoring Programme.* Cambridge: Pearson Publishing.

Furlong, J. and Maynard, T. (1995) *Mentoring Student Teachers: The Growth of Professional Knowledge.* London and New York: Routledge.

Furlong, V., Hirst, P., Pocklington, K. and Miles, S. (1988) *Initial Teacher Training and the Role of the Schools.* Buckingham: Open University Press.

Galvez-Hjornevik, C. (1985) *Teacher Mentors: A Review of the Literature.* Austin: Texas University Research and Development.

Gardiner, J. (1998) 'Teaching as a career? Yes, but . . . ' *Times Educational Supplement,* 13 March.

Gardner, W. and Libde, A. (1995) 'Professional development schools: how well will they travel?' *Journal of Education for Teaching*, **21**(3), 303–15.

Garrigan, P. and Strivens, J. (1991) 'A profile in perspective: the record of professional development for student teachers at Liverpool University.' In Whiteman (1992).

Gifford, S. (1992) 'Surrey New Teacher Competency Project.' *British Journal of In-Service Education*, **18**(3).

Goddard, D. (1993) 'The role of the LEA in induction.' *British Journal of In-Service Education*, **19**(1), 46–54.

Godley, L. B. (1987) 'The teacher consultant role: impact on the profession.' *Action in Teacher Education*, **8**(4).

Goodman, J. (1987) 'Factors in becoming a pro-active elementary school teacher: a preliminary study of selected novices.' *Journal of Education for Teaching*, **13**(3).

Grant, C. and Zeichner, K. (1981) 'In-service support for first year teachers: the state of the scene.' *Journal of Research Development in Education*, **14**(2).

Graves, N. (ed.) (1990) *Initial Teacher Education*. London: Kogan Page.

Gray, J. (1996) *Merging Traditions: The Future of Research on School Effectiveness and School Improvement*. London: Cassell.

Greenes, C. E. (1994) 'The partnership: the history.' *The Journal of Education*, **176**(1), 9–19.

Greiner-Makin, S. (1996) 'Why is the "duckling" preferable to the "parrot" as a teacher? Four beginning teacher types.' *European Journal of Teacher Education*, **19**(1), 13–18.

Griffin, P. E. (1982) 'The developing confidence of new teachers.' *Journal of Education for Teaching*, **9**(2), 113–22.

Griffiths, V. and Owen, P. (eds) (1995) *Schools in Partnership*. London: Paul Chapman.

Guri-Rozenblit, S. (1990) 'Four models of teacher training in Israel: some lessons and implications for teacher educators.' *Journal of Education for Teaching*, **16**(3), 225–33.

Guri-Rozenblit, S. (1995) 'Collaboration between teacher training colleges and the Open University of Israel.' *Teacher Education*, Fall/Winter, **74**, 59–67.

Hagger, H., Burn, K. and McIntyre, D. (1995) *The School Mentor Handbook: Essential Skills and Strategies for Working with Student Teachers*. London: Kogan Page.

Haigh, G. (1991) 'Visible means of support.' *Times Educational Supplement*, 26 April.

Hake, C. (1993) *Partnership in Initial Teacher Training: Talk and Chalk*. London: Tufnell Press.

Hall, G. E. (ed.) (1982) 'Induction: the missing link.' *Journal of Teacher Education*, **33**(3).

Hall, G. et al. (1982) *Beginning Teacher Induction: Five Dilemmas*, Proceedings from a Public Forum. Texas: University of Texas at Austin.

Hammond, G. (ed.) (1976) *The First Year of Teaching* (Paper 37). Exeter: Exeter School of Education.

Hargreaves, D. H. (1994) *Development Planning for School Improvement*. London: Cassell.

Heath-Camp, B. and Camp, W. (1990) 'What new teachers need to succeed.' *Vocational Education Journal*, **65**(4).

Hegarty, P. and Simco, N. (1995) 'Partnership and progress: teacher mentoring in United Kingdom teacher education (primary).' *Action in Teacher Education*, **17**(2).

Hogben, D. and Lawson, M. J. (1984) 'Trainee and beginning teacher attitude stability and change: four case studies.' *Journal of Education for Teaching*, **10**(2), 135–56.

Holmes Group (1986) *Tomorrow's Teachers*. East Lancing, MI: The Holmes Group.

Holmes Group (1990) *Tomorrow's Schools*. East Lancing, MI: The Holmes Group.

Hopkins, D. (1994) *School Improvement in an Era of Change*. London: Cassell.

Houston, W. R. and Felder, B. (1982) 'Break horses not teachers.' *Phi Delta Kappan*, **63**(7).

Huffman, G. and Leak, S. (1986) 'Beginning teachers' perceptions of mentors.' *Journal of Teacher Education*, **37**(1), 22–5.

Hughes, E. C. (1975) 'Professions.' In G. N. Esland, J. G. Salaman and N. Speakman (eds) *People and Work*. Edinburgh: Holmes-McDougal/Oxford University Press.

Huling-Austin, L. (1986) 'What can and what cannot reasonably be expected from teacher induction programmes?' *Journal of Teacher Education*, **37**(1), 2–5.

Hunter, J. (1988) 'Induction of new teachers: an annotated bibliography'. Indiana University Exit Project ERIC DOC ED304428.

Husen, T. and Postlethwaite, N. (eds) (1984) *International Encyclopedia of Educational Research*. Oxford: Pergamon Press.

Hutchinson, B. (1982) 'Action research for professional development and the improvement of schooling.' In Elliot, J. and Whitehead, D. (1982) *Action Research for Professional Development and the Improvement of Schooling*. Cambridge: Cambridge Institute of Education.

Jaworski, B. (1993) *Mentoring in Mathematics Teaching*. London: Falmer Press.

Jennings, S. (1994) *Introduction to Mentoring in Teacher Education*. Exeter: University of Exeter.

Jordell, K. O. (1987) 'Structural and personal influences in the socialization of beginning teachers.' *Teaching and Teacher Education*, **3**(3).

Kerry, T. and Mayes, A. S. (eds) (1995) *Issues in Mentoring*. London and New York: Routledge for Open University.

Kremer-Hayon, L. (1987) 'Perceived teaching difficulties of beginning teachers.' *Research in Education*, **37**.

Lacey, C. (1977) *The Socialisation of Teachers*. London: Methuen.

Lawlor, S. (1990) *Teachers Mistaught: Training in Theories or Education in Subjects?* London: Centre for Policy Studies.

Lee, N. and Crouch, H. (1993) 'Report on survey of Year 1 and Year 2 B.Ed. students' use of professional profiles.' Brentwood: Anglia Polytechnic University (unpublished).

Littleton, P. and Littleton, M. (1988) 'Induction programmes for beginning teachers.' *The Clearing House*, **62**, September.

Lortie, D. (1975) *Schoolteacher*. Chicago: Chicago University Press.

Marson, R. N. and Pigge, F. L. (1988) 'The differences between self-perceived job expectations and job realities of beginning teachers.' *Journal of Teacher Education*, **38**(6).

Maude, P. and Turner, M. (1993) 'The Essex partnership for the induction of newly qualified teachers.' Paper delivered to the British Educational Research Conference at Oxford.

Maw, J. (1975) 'Professional tutor or teacher: what's in a name?' *British Journal of In-Service Education*, **2**(1).

McCabe, C. (1978) 'A new look at the problems of the probationary teacher.' *British Journal of In-Service Education*, **4**(3).

McCabe, C. and Woodward, K. (1982) 'Induction in reduced circumstances.' *British Journal of In-Service Education*, **9**(2).

McDonald, F. J. et al. (1980) *A Study of Induction Programs for Beginning Teachers* (3 vols). Princeton, NJ: Educational Testing Service.

McIntyre, D. and Byrd, D. (eds) (1996) *Preparing Tomorrow's Teachers: The Field Experience*. Thousand Oaks, CA: Corwin Press.

McIntyre, D., Hagger, H. and Wilkin, M. (eds) (1993) *Mentoring: Perspectives on School-based Teacher Education*. London: Kogan Page.

McMahon, A. (1976) 'Visiting tutor roles.' *British Journal of In-Service Education*, **2**(3).

McMahon, A. (1981) 'The role of the school-based tutor in the professional development of teachers.' *Journal of Education*, Spring.

McMahon, A. and Bolam, R. (1981) *TIPS Survey of LEA Induction Schemes*. Bristol: University of Bristol School of Education.

McNamara, D. (1995) 'The influence of student teachers, tutors and mentors upon their classroom practice: an exploratory study.' *Teaching and Teacher Education*, **2**(1), 54–61.

McPake, J., Powney, J., Somekh, B., Biott, C., Edward, S. and Spindler, J. (1997) *Career*

Entry Profiles 1996: Evaluation of the Teacher Training Agency Pilot: Executive Summary. Scottish Council for Research in Education with University of Northumbria at Newcastle.

Ministry of Education (1959) *Probation of Teachers,* Statutory Instrument 364.

Moon, B. and Mayes, A. S. (1994) *Teaching and Learning in the Secondary School.* London: Routledge.

Moreira, J. (1996) 'Approaches to teacher professional development: a critical appraisal.' *European Journal of Teacher Education,* **19**(1), 47–63.

Mortimore, P. (1990) *Building the Bridge: Profiling the Student Teacher. A New Approach to Assessment.* Conference proceedings, 26–27 January, Viking Hotel, York.

Myers, C. B. (1996) 'Beyond the PDS: schools as professional learning communities.' Paper presented at American Educational Research Association Meeting, New York.

Myers, K. (1995) *School Improvement in Practice: Schools Make a Difference Project.* London: Falmer Press.

National Committee for Accreditation of Teacher Training (1996) *NCATE PDS Standards Project Preliminary Survey Findings.*

National Council for Vocational Qualifications (1986) *Review of Vocational Qualifications.*

Nias, J. (1984) 'Learning and acting the roles: in school support for primary teachers.' *Educational Review,* **36**(1).

Norris, N. (1991) 'The trouble with competence.' *Cambridge Journal of Education,* **21**(3), 331–41.

O'Hear, A. (1988) *Who Teaches the Teachers?* London: Social Affairs Unit.

Odell, S. J. (1986) 'Induction support of new teachers: a functional approach.' *Journal of Teacher Education,* **37**(1).

Odell, S. J. and Ferarro, D. P. (1992) 'Teacher mentoring and teacher retention.' *Journal of Teacher Education,* **43**(3).

Office for Standards in Education (1993a) *The Government's Proposals for the Reform of Initial Teacher Training* ('Blue Paper'). London: HMSO.

Office for Standards in Education (1993b) *The New Teacher in School 1992.* London: HMSO.

Office for Standards in Education (1993c) *The Training of Primary School Teachers, March 1991 to March 1992.* London: HMSO.

Office for Standards in Education (1995) *School-centred Initial Teacher Training 1993–1994.* London: HMSO.

Owen, J. C. (1968) 'Strategies of curriculum innovation.' *Journal of Curriculum Studies,* **1**(1).

Parsloe, E. (1995) *Coaching, Mentoring and Assessing: A Practical Guide to Developing Competence.* London: Kogan Page (revised edn).

Patrick, H., Bernbaum, G. and Reid, K. (1984) 'The P.G.C.E. and the probationary year.' *British Journal of In-Service Education,* **10**(3).

Pedlar, M., Boydell, T. and Burgoyne, J. (1989) 'Towards the learning company.' *Management Education and Development,* **20**(1).

Phares, E. J. (1976) *Locus of Control in Personality.* New Jersey: General Learning Press.

Pollard, A. and Tann, S. (1987) *Reflective Teaching in the Primary School.* London: Cassell (3rd edn 1997).

Pollard, A. and Tann, S. (1993) *Reflective Teaching in the Primary School: A Handbook for the Classroom.* London: Cassell (2nd edn).

Pomeroy, R. (1993) 'Mentorship training: the current picture.' *Mentoring,* **1**(2).

Pritchard, K. J. (1987) 'Profiles and records of achievement in initial teacher education.' In Schön, D. (1987)

Probert, R., Maisch, M. and Winter, R. (1992) *The ASSET Model of Professional Development.* Chelmsford: Anglia Polytechnic and Essex County Council.

Quaglia, R. (1989) 'Socialization of the beginning teacher: a theoretical model from the empirical literature.' *Research in Rural Education*, **5**(3).

Reid, I., Constable, H. and Griffiths, R. (1995) *Teacher Education Reform*. London: Paul Chapman.

Reid, K., Bullock, R. and Howarth, S. (1988) *An Introduction to Primary School Organisation*. London: Hodder & Stoughton.

Rosenholtz, S. J. (1989) 'Workplace conditions that affect teacher quality and commitment: implications for teacher induction practices.' *Elementary School Journal*, **89**(4).

Rotter, J. (1966) 'Generalized expectancies for internal v. external control of reinforcement.' *Psychological Reports*, **80**, 609.

Ruddock, J. (1995) *School Improvement: What Can Pupils Tell Us?* London: David Fulton.

Ryan, K. (1970) 'Stages of induction.' In Ryan, K. (ed.) *Don't Smile until Christmas*. Chicago: University of Chicago Press.

Ryan, K., Newman, K. K., Mager, G., Applegate, J. H., Lasley, T., Flora, U. R. and Johnson, J. (1980) *Biting the Apple*. New York: Longman.

Ryan, K. (1982) 'Why bother with induction?' In Hall, G. *et al.* (1982).

Ryan, K. (1986) *The Induction of New Teachers*. Bloomington, IN: Phi Delta Kappa Education Foundation.

Schön, D. A. (1983) *The Reflective Practitioner: How Professionals Think in Action*. New York: Basic Books.

Schön, D. (1987) *Educating the Reflective Practitioner*. London: Jossey-Bass.

Sears, D. A. (1994) 'The partnership – the present.' *The Journal of Education*, **176**(1), 21–6.

Sellars, B. and Crowther, K. (1977) 'The professional staff tutor role.' *Journal of Applied Educational Studies*, **6**(2).

Shaw, R. (1992) *Teacher Training in Secondary Schools*. London: Kogan Page.

Shea, G. F. (1992) *Mentoring*. London: Kogan Page.

Skilbeck, M. (1982) 'Probation and the inspector.' *Times Educational Supplement*, 5 November.

Skinner, P. (ed.) (1993) *Individual Action Planning and the National Record of Achievement in the Continuous Professional Development of School Staff*. Leicester: Leicester University (Conference report).

Smith, P. and West-Burnham, J. (1993) *Mentoring in the Effective School*. Harlow: Longman.

Smith, T. R. (1992) *Second to None: A Vision of a New California High School*. Sacramento, CA: California Department of Education.

Smyth, K. and McCabe, C. (1980) *Induction on a Reduced Budget*. Newcastle: School of Education, Newcastle-upon-Tyne.

Smyth, K. and McCabe, C. (1981) *Induction in Northumberland: Induction on a Budget II*. Newcastle: School of Education, University of Newcastle-upon-Tyne.

Spooner, R. (1984) 'The art of the confidence trickster.' *Education*, 20 January.

Stallings, J. and Kowalski, T. (1990) 'Research on professional development schools.' In Houston, W. R. (ed.) *Handbook of Research on Teacher Education*. New York: Macmillan, pp. 251–63.

Stephens, P. (1996) *Essential Mentoring Skills: A Practical Handbook for School-based Teacher Educators*. Cheltenham: Stanley Thornes.

Stone, B. (1987) 'Why teachers fail.' *Principal*, September.

Stones, E. (1987) 'Teaching practice supervision: bridge between theory and practice.' *European Journal of Teacher Education*, **10**(1).

Taylor, J. K. and Dale, I. R. (1973) 'The first year of teaching.' In Lomax, D. (ed.) *The Education of Teachers in Britain*. London: J. Wiley & Sons.

Teacher Training Agency (1997) 'Revised requirements for all courses of initial teacher training (Paper 1).' In *Training Curriculum and Standards for New Teachers*. London: TTA.

Teitel, L. (1994) 'Can school–university partnerships lead to the simultaneous renewal of schools and teacher education?' *Journal of Teacher Education*, **45**(4), 245–52.

Teitel, L. (1996) 'Separations, divorces and open marriages in professional development school partnerships.' Paper at American Educational Research Association Meeting, New York.

Thompson, M. (1991) 'Competencies: the implications for training courses.' Paper delivered to UCET annual conference.

Thompson, M. (1993) 'The weakest link: the ATL's proposals.' *British Journal of In-Service Education*, **19**(1), 12–15.

Tickle, L. (1988) 'New teachers and the development of professionalism.' In Holly, M. L. and McLoughlin, C. S. (eds) (1988) *Perspectives on Professional Teacher Development*. Lewes: Falmer Press.

Tickle, L. (1989) 'On probation: preparation for professionalism.' *Cambridge Journal of Education*, **19**(3).

Tickle, L. (1994) *The Induction of New Teachers: Reflective Professional Practice*. London and New York: Cassell.

Tisher, R. P. (1979) *Teacher Induction: An Aspect of the Education and Professional Development of Teachers*. Austin: University of Texas Research and Development Centre.

Tisher, R. P. (1982) 'Teacher induction: an international perspective.' Paper given at the New York meeting of the American Educational Research Association.

Tomlinson, P. (1995) *Understanding Mentoring: Reflective Strategies for School-based Teacher Preparation*. Buckingham: Open University Press.

Tomlinson, P. and Saunders, S. (1994) Correspondence re. research project, University of Leeds. Unpublished.

Trethowan, D. M. and Smith, D. L. (1985) *Induction of New Staff into Schools*. London: The Industrial Society.

Turner, M. A. (1982) 'The deep end.' *Times Educational Supplement*, No. 3461, 29 November.

Turner, M. A. (1983) *Problems of Teachers of English in their Probationary Year* (Occasional Research Paper No. 7). Brentwood: Chelmer Institute of Higher Education.

Turner, M. A. (1992) 'The management of the probation and induction of teachers in primary schools.' University of Sussex D.Phil. thesis, (Unpublished).

Turner, M. A. (1993a) 'The complementary roles of the headteacher, the mentor and the advisory teacher in school-based teacher training.' *Mentoring*, **1**(2).

Turner, M. A. (1993b) 'The role of mentors and teacher tutors in school-based teacher education and induction.' *British Journal of In-Service Education*, **19**(1).

Turner, M. A. (1994) 'The management of the induction of newly qualified teachers in primary schools.' *Journal of Education for Teaching*, **20**(3).

Turner, M. A. (1995) 'The role of mentors and teacher tutors in school-based teacher education and induction.' In Kerry and Mayes (1995).

Varah, L. J., Theune, W. S. and Parker, L. (1986) 'Beginning teachers, sink or swim.' *Journal of Teacher Education*, **37**(1).

Veenman, S. (1984) 'Perceived problems of the beginning teacher.' *Review of Educational Research*, **54**(2).

Vonk, J. H. C. (1983) 'The problems of the beginning teacher.' *European Journal of Teacher Education*, **6**(2).

Waite, D. (1995) *Rethinking Instructional Supervision*. London: Falmer Press.

Wall, M. and Smith, P. (1993) *Mentoring Programme*. Manchester: Manchester Metropolitan University.

Wallace, R. C. (1982) 'Teacher induction: who is responsible?' In Hall, G. et al. (1982).

Waller, W. (1932) *The Sociology of Teaching*. New York: John Wiley.

Wanous, J. P. (1980) *Organisational Entry*. Reading, MA: Addison Wesley Publishing.

Watkins, C. and Whalley, C. (1993) 'Mentoring beginning teachers: issues for schools to anticipate and manage.' *School Organisation*, **13**(2).

Whiteman, S. (ed.) (1992) *What's IT All About?* Birmingham: Newman College.

Whitty, G. and Willmott, E. (1991) 'Competency based teacher education: issues and concerns.' *Cambridge Journal of Education*, **21**(3).

Wideen, M. and Andrews, I. H. (1987) *Staff Development for Staff Improvement*. Lewes: Falmer Press.

Wildman, T. M., Niles, J., Maglario, S. and McLaughlin, R. (1987) 'Teaching and learning to teach: the two roles of the elementary school teacher.' *The Elementary School Journal*, **89**(4).

Wilkin, M. (ed.) (1992) *Mentoring in Schools*. London: Kogan Page.

Wilkin, M. and Sankey, D. (eds) (1994) *Collaboration and Transition in Initial Teacher Training*. London: Kogan Page.

Williams, A. (1993) 'Teacher perceptions of their needs in the context of developing school-based initial teacher education.' *British Educational Research Journal*, **19**(4).

Wilson, J. and D'Arcy, J. M. (1987) 'Employment conditions and induction opportunities.' *European Journal of Education*, **10**(2).

Winter, R. and Maisch, M. (1991) *Professionalism and Competence: Conference Papers*. Chelmsford: Anglia Polytechnic and Essex County Council Social Services.

Winter, R. and Powney, J. (1988) 'Teacher education and the accreditation of individual learning.' *Journal of Further and Higher Education*, **12**(3).

Wubbels, T., Creton, H. A. and Hooymayer, H. P. (1987) 'A school-based teacher induction programme.' *European Journal of Education*, **10**(1).

Yeomans, R. and Sampson, J. (eds) (1994) *Mentorship in the Primary School*. London and Washington, DC: Falmer Press.

Zeichner, K. (1979) *Teacher Induction Practices in the United States and Great Britain*. Wisconsin: Department of Curriculum and Instruction.

Zeichner, K. (1992) 'Rethinking the practicum in the professional development school.' *Journal of Teacher Education*, **43**(4), 296–307.

Zeichner, K. (1995) 'Beyond the divide of teacher research and academic research.' *Teachers and Teaching*, **1**(2), 153–72.

Zeichner, K. and Tabachnick, B. (1985) 'The development of teacher perspectives, social strategies and institutional control in the socialization of beginning teachers.' *Journal of Education for Teaching*, **11**(1).

Index

NC02422

THE NORTHERN COLLEGE
LIBRARY
8079
BARNSLEY